50 YEARS
lonely planet
OF TRAVEL

BEST IN TRAVEL 2024

The best destinations, journeys and experiences, for the year ahead

CONTENTS

Top 10 Regions

Top 10 Sustainable

Top 10 Best Value

1 The Vltava River from Letná Park, Prague

2 Taking a break on the Mongolian steppes

INTRODUCTION
by Tom Hall

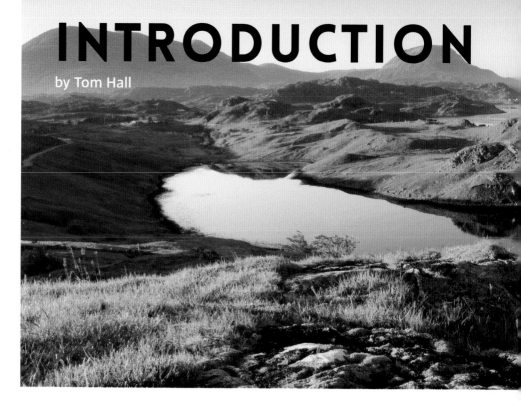

The promise behind *Across Asia on the Cheap*, the book that launched Lonely Planet in 1973, was making possible an incredible adventure across a world waiting to be discovered. In this and so many subsequent guidebooks, our founders Tony and Maureen Wheeler shared a vision that you could fulfil your travel dreams, and that unique experiences, people and perspectives awaited around every corner. If you read carefully, you can also learn that omelettes with mind-altering ingredients were available in Bali: this was 1973 after all.

Fifty years on, Lonely Planet's *Best in Travel 2024* builds on this legacy of inspiring future journeys, near and far, with fifty destinations, journeys and experiences.

As you may expect if you've seen *Best in Travel* in print and online before, many of the suggestions are based on countries, regions and cities. While all of our selections place great emphasis on experiences celebrating community, sustainability and diversity, we've included a specific list of top sustainable travel destinations. We've also included a list of best-value destinations to show how you can travel well in a world of rising costs.

Compiling *Best in Travel* is a team effort that seeks to collect and distil the wisdom of writers, editors and everyone else at Lonely Planet. This year we were able to benefit from the expertise of many locally based contributors who have added to our

new Experience guides and our iconic, re-envisaged guidebooks. Perhaps it was bound up in the enthusiasm for travel, but we had enough fantastic suggestions to fill this book many times over. Our panel of travel experts and writers from around the world then ranked these lists for topicality, uniqueness and that wow factor that merits a place in *Best in Travel*. As ever, we'd love your thoughts on what we've got right, and what we may have missed.

Top of the class for 2024 are the untamed open lands of Mongolia, bike-touring on the Trans Dinarica Cycling Route across the western

1 Loch Inchard, in Scotland's far-north Flow Country

Balkans, and diving into one of Africa's most dynamic cities, Nairobi in Kenya. A sustainable travel guide to Spain and a budget-friendly adventure in the USA's Midwest complete the headline acts. There are also many more suggestions spanning the globe, from Donegal in Ireland's windswept northwest to the spectacular deserts of Algeria, Kangaroo Island's raw native nature, and jungle-framed beaches on St Lucia.

Since Lonely Planet last published *Best in Travel*, travel has well and truly bounced back. For some travellers, first steps in these journeys have seen tentative, testing times both literal and logistical, moving round a world grappling with how to open up again. But it's been worth it: many have relished every opportunity to shake off the dust of lockdown and experience first-hand both the wonders of the return of travel and the frustrations of an entire industry racing to get up to speed with demand. Good and bad, it's been a trip in itself.

Our picks for this year seek to both inspire and follow the instincts of the post-pandemic traveller. A traveller who aims for

THE BEST IN TRAVEL PROMISE

WHERE IS THE BEST PLACE TO VISIT RIGHT NOW?

This is the most hotly contested topic at Lonely Planet. As self-confessed travel geeks, our global community of staff and writers roams widely most years, exploring almost every destination on the planet in the process.

Where is the best place to visit right now? We ask everyone at Lonely Planet, from our writers and editors all the way to our online family of social media influencers. And each year they come up with hundreds of places that are special right now, offer new things for travellers to see or do, or are overlooked and underrated.

Amid fierce debate, the list is whittled down by our panel of travel experts to just 10 countries, 10 regions, 10 cities, 10 best value destinations and 10 top sustainable destinations. Each is chosen for its topicality, unique experiences and 'wow' factor.

Put simply, what remains in the pages that follow is the cream of this year's travel picks, courtesy of Lonely Planet: 10 countries, 10 regions, 10 cities, 10 best value destinations and 10 top sustainable destinations to inspire you to explore for yourself.

So what are you waiting for?

unique experiences, to engage with a changing world, be aware of their impact and prize every single journey. With a nod to countries indelibly associated with the Lonely Planet story, we're revisiting India, Thailand and Kenya. We're also excited to bring picks like Nicaragua, Benin and Uzbekistan that have rarely, if ever, been in the series.

Our suggestions also aim to give fresh takes on popular themes. Enjoy hiking? Consider the Portuguese Camino de Santiago, and the trail system throughout Wales, which has spent much of this year shaping itself as even more of a remarkable walking destination than before. The thrilling renaissance of night trains in Europe remains the best way to combine sleeping with an unforgettable journey and is still very much on-trend among the climate-conscious. Rediscovering old favourites? It feels as refreshing as a dip in Lake Wānaka to herald a

return to the Central Otago region of New Zealand (Aotearoa).

Travel remains a privilege, with ethnicity and nationality determining whether your journey can be made on a whim or is necessary for survival. Desperation drives dangerous journeys. Many depend on transport links to escape conflict zones and other dangers the world over. In years to come, we would love to once again wholeheartedly recommend returning to some much-loved destinations and experiences that currently cannot be visited due to instability and conflict. In the meantime, consider setting aside some of your travel budget to support those impacted by conflict and natural disaster.

For the lucky ones, 2024 is a year of huge, thrilling possibility. The final word before hitting the road should go to *Across Asia on the Cheap*: 'All you've got to do is decide to go and the hardest part is over. So go.'

2 Peeking at the Pitons in St Lucia **3** Handpainted furniture in Tangier, Morocco **4** Serene Lake McDonald in Glacier National Park, USA

Far North Scotland

Donegal

NORTH
PACIFIC
OCEAN

País Vasco

Montana

Montréal

NORTH AMERICA

Morocco

Kansas City

Philadelphia

NORTH
ATLANTIC
OCEAN

Mexico

St Lucia

Manaus

SOUTH
AMERICA

Chile

SOUTH
PACIFIC
OCEAN

SOUTH
ATLANTIC
OCEAN

Best countries
Best cities
Best regions

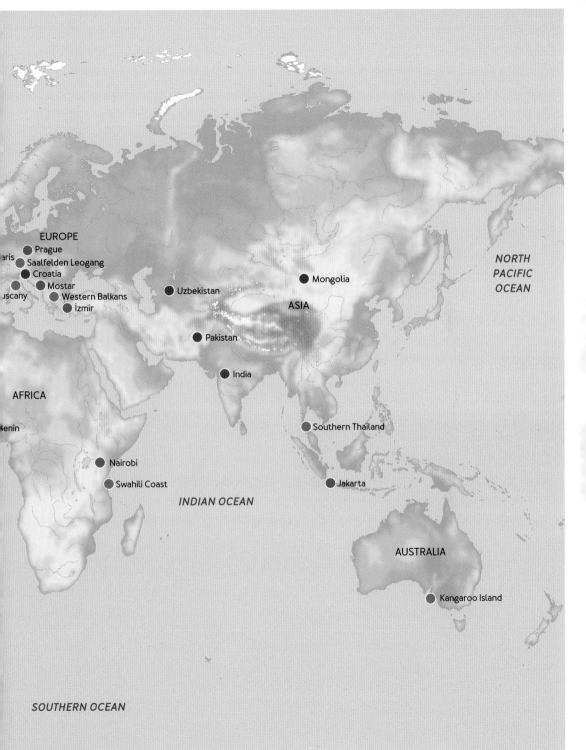

EUROPE
- Paris
- Prague
- Saalfelden Leogang
- Croatia
- Mostar
- Tuscany
- Western Balkans
- İzmir

Uzbekistan

Mongolia

ASIA

Pakistan

India

AFRICA
- Benin

Nairobi

Swahili Coast

Southern Thailand

Jakarta

INDIAN OCEAN

NORTH PACIFIC OCEAN

AUSTRALIA

Kangaroo Island

SOUTHERN OCEAN

9

LONELY PLANET'S

BEST IN TRAVEL 2024
TOP 10
COUNTRIES

Mongolia / India / Morocco / Chile / Benin
Mexico / Uzbekistan / Pakistan / Croatia / St Lucia

MONGOLIA

01

For seekers of wide-open spaces, adventures and culture, Mongolia has much to offer. The capital is a 180-degree contrast: a big city teeming with people and unique attractions. Squeezed between Russia and China, Mongolia seems hard to reach given recent geopolitical events in its two large neighbours. But Mongolia's doors are open and a tourism campaign has eased visa restrictions through 2025.

Reopening doors

Mongolia roared back to life after two challenging pandemic years that shut down the economy and tourism. Bars, restaurants and nightclubs are now abuzz as locals shake off the cobwebs and get back to having fun. City

1 Anton Petrus/Getty Images © 2 Taylor Weidman/Getty Images ©

3 Michal Vit/Shutterstock ©

Highlights

01 **Hear the magical sounds** of the Tumen Ekh Ensemble, a traditional music group that performs in Ulaanbaatar nightly in summer.

02 **Try a traditional dinner** of steamed dumplings prepared by a nomad family on the steppes.

03 **Get up close** to the action at a countryside Naadam where local athletes compete for prizes in horse racing, archery and wrestling.

04 **Saddle up and ride** into the mountains on a Mongolian horse, the breed that helped Chinggis Khaan conquer much of Eurasia.

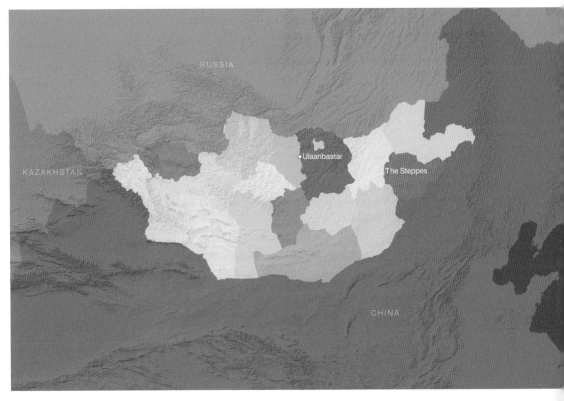

dwellers have also poured into the countryside to enjoy the open spaces, lakes and rivers – a welcome respite after months of quarantine. Now the government wants foreign visitors to return too, and has declared 2023 and 2024 as 'Years to Visit Mongolia'. One of its initiatives will exempt citizens of 34 countries from visa requirements for up to 30 days until the end of 2025. Most of Europe is included, along with Australia and New Zealand. This is on top of the 27 countries that already enjoyed visa-free travel, including the United States. To help boost visitor numbers, Mongolian Airlines (MIAT) is planning a non-stop flight to the US. For European travellers, there are direct connections with Frankfurt and İstanbul. Since 2021, flights have been arriving at Ulaanbaatar's new Chinggis Khaan International Airport, located 50km (31 miles) south of the capital.

Capital sights

Once on the ground in Ulaanbaatar, make your first stop the Chinggis Khaan National Museum, unveiled in 2022. Covering the breadth of Mongolian history, it culminates with the reign of Chinggis Khaan (Genghis Khan), the great 13th-century Mongol warrior who founded the world's largest single land empire. Next, stroll downtown and take in some of the new parks and street-improvement projects put in place by Ulaanbaatar's mayor, a two-time Olympic wrestler turned politician. For an

15

I love the Mongolian countryside. There I feel no time pressure, just a feeling of space and tranquillity. Especially in the Gobi Desert or the steppe, my stress instantly vanishes.

Oyungerel Tsedevdamba, author

off-the-beaten-path adventure, head for the Golden Eagle Festival (scheduled for 14–15 September 2024), located 1600km west of Ulaanbaatar. This event features ethnic Kazakhs who use eagles to hunt mock prey in a colourful competition, made famous by the 2016 documentary, *The Eagle Huntress*.

North and south

Venturing out of Ulaanbaatar still requires travel along some of Mongolia's famously rough roads, but recently built highways will speed up transport across the country. By 2024, a new four-lane highway north to Darkhan should be complete, shortening travel time to northern Mongolia. Heading south is also a wise choice to glimpse the new Gobi Museum of Nature and History in Dalanzadgad. The Gobi is famed for its dinosaur fossils and these are beautifully displayed here. The centrepiece is a *Tarbosaurus bataar*, a cousin of the T-Rex. Travellers heading to the ancient capital of Kharkhorin can stop in at the city's newly built Erdenesiin Khuree Mongolian Calligraphy Center, which functions as a gallery where visitors can watch artists produce amazing works of calligraphic art.

Tradition rules

New museums and attractions help visitors better understand the country, but to really appreciate Mongolia one must venture into the open steppes. You'll likely meet the nomad families who tend their livestock here, and might be offered fresh yoghurt if you pitch your tent for the night near one of their camps. A jeep trip across the countryside may also include stops at a local Naadam festival, complete with horse racing, archery and wrestling.

1 Tsambagarav Uul National Park, in the Altai Mountains of the far west 2 A *morin khuur* player at Ulaanbaatar's Choijin Lama Temple 3 The fast-growing capital 4 Camping in the Gobi Desert, under the Milky Way 5 Buddhist imagery at the Choijin Lama Temple 6 Hunting with golden eagles

Getting there

Ulaanbaatar's new airport is the quickest way in. Covid cancelled train travel from Beijing, but this route may restart by 2024.

When to go

Mongolia is best visited in the summer when the steppes turn electric green and you can explore the countryside. July is the main time to catch Naadam events happening in small towns across the country. August is optimal for good weather.

Further reading

For life and culture, read *Dateline Mongolia* by Michael Kohn. *Genghis Khan and the Making of the Modern World* by Jack Weatherford provides historical context.

02

INDIA

After some tough years for travel, India is back on the map, with new flight routes providing easy access from Europe and America to much-loved hubs such as Delhi, Mumbai, Goa and Kerala, and new transport links in the Northeast States. India's railways are also in for a revamp, with stylish new trains rolling out across the network. For travellers itching for a dose of dosas and a top-up of temples, it's the ideal time to get back to the world's most colourful country.

Fast ways into India

With the bursting of India's private airline bubble – and the exit of major carriers such as Kingfisher and Jet Airways – direct flights to India were dwindling, but the national carrier, Air

1 Matt Munro/Lonely Planet © 2 Nicholas Pitt/Getty Images ©

Highlights

01 **Touring India's temples,** from Khajuraho's erotic carvings to the rainbow-coloured *gopurams* (gateway towers) of the south.

02 **Himalayan encounters** – northern India is a world crowned by mountains, dotted with hill stations and crossed by trekking trails.

03 **Feasting on a cuisine** that's as varied and nuanced as Indian culture, drawing on the world's most extravagant palette of spices.

04 **Market mayhem** – bazaars such as Delhi's Chandni Chowk are an intense introduction to India's sights, sounds and smells.

3 rchphoto/Getty Images ©

India, is back in expansion mode, with new non-stop flights from cities across the globe.

In 2024, it will be easier than ever to get from European hubs such as Gatwick, Milan and Vienna to Goa's blissful beaches or Delhi's brilliant bazaars without extra, carbon-intensive takeoffs and landings along the way. Visitors from the US can reach Mumbai, Delhi and Bengaluru in a single leg, while travellers looking for an easy passage to India can skip frenetic Delhi for gentler hubs such as Ahmedabad, Kochi and Amritsar.

Flying into smaller cities is the low-stress way to arrive in the subcontinent, with less competition for hotels and transport and easy access to less-explored parts of the country. Try flying into Amritsar as a back route to mountain-circled Himachal Pradesh and Ladakh, or explore underappreciated Gujarat from Ahmedabad as an alternative to mobbed Rajasthan.

Easier travel by rail and river

India's railways were once the pride of the nation, but the network has been looking a little shabby in recent years, with threadbare carriages

1 The ghats of Varanasi run down to the Ganges **2** Mealtime in Goa **3** Houseboats ply the backwaters of Kerala **4** A tea plantation in Munnar **5** Whitewater rafting on the Ganges in Rishikesh, in the Himalayan foothills **6** The historic Chinese-style fishing nets are an icon of the southern port city of Kochi

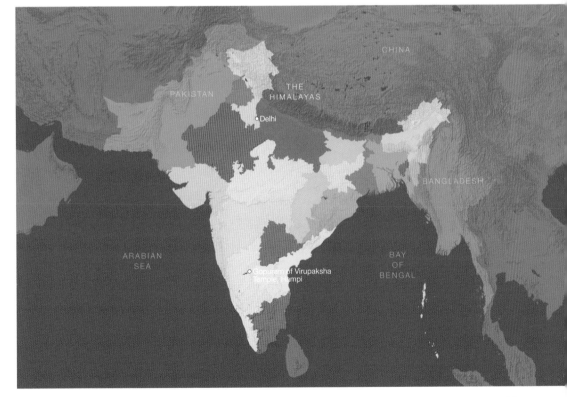

> *To get a real taste of India, I would go to the market in Old Delhi and order tea from a local tea vendor, then take a cycle-rickshaw through the backstreets to buy spices.*

Nadeem Sheikh, travel agent, Delhi

and creaky rolling stock. Here's the good news: the railways are back, with new investment in cutting-edge trains that are set to transform the Indian train-travel experience.

Streamlined new Vande Bharat engines and carriages are being rolled out on city-to-city and suburban routes across the country, cutting journey times by hours on key routes and maximising comfort – rotating chairs in Executive Class and airline-style vacuum loos anyone?

Even if you miss out on the new locos, rail infrastructure is improving everywhere, meaning more comfort as you roll from the Himalayan foothills to the southern beaches. Plan at least one long-distance rail journey as part of your trip – there's no experience quite like waking up on an Indian sleeper train barrelling across the plains.

If boats are more your speed, consider a trip on the MV *Ganges Vilas*, which follows the Ganges, Brahmaputra and other mighty waterways for nearly 2000 miles through India and Bangladesh on the world's longest river cruise.

Connected capitals in the northeast

Connected only tenuously to the rest of the country, the seven Northeast States have always

been India's wild frontier. But visiting the region's mountain villages, thundering waterfalls, living rope bridges and 145 tribal communities is about to get a whole lot easier.

The Indian government has launched a new action plan to connect all the state capitals – Guwahati (Assam), Shillong (Meghalaya), Itanagar (Arunachal Pradesh), Kohima (Nagaland), Imphal (Manipur), Aizawl (Mizoram) and Agartala (Tripura) – with new rail and air routes from Delhi by 2025.

This means now is the sweet spot for visiting the Northeast, before the world takes notice of these mesmerising mountains, culture-rich communities and wildlife-filled jungles. From Himalayan valleys studded with Buddhist monasteries to dense tropical rainforests dotted with grass-thatched stilt homes, it's India, but not as you know it.

Getting there

Flight routes fan out across the globe. Depending on cross-border politics, it may be possible to travel overland from Pakistan to Rajasthan, or from Tibet in China to northern India via Nepal, but always check the security situation beforehand.

When to go

Avoid the rain-drenched monsoon from May to September (unless you're heading to Ladakh). For the rest of India, the dry, cooler winter, from October to April, is ideal.

Further reading

Start with *Midnight's Children* by Salman Rushdie; *A Fine Balance* by Rohinton Mistry; and *The God of Small Things* by Arundhati Roy.

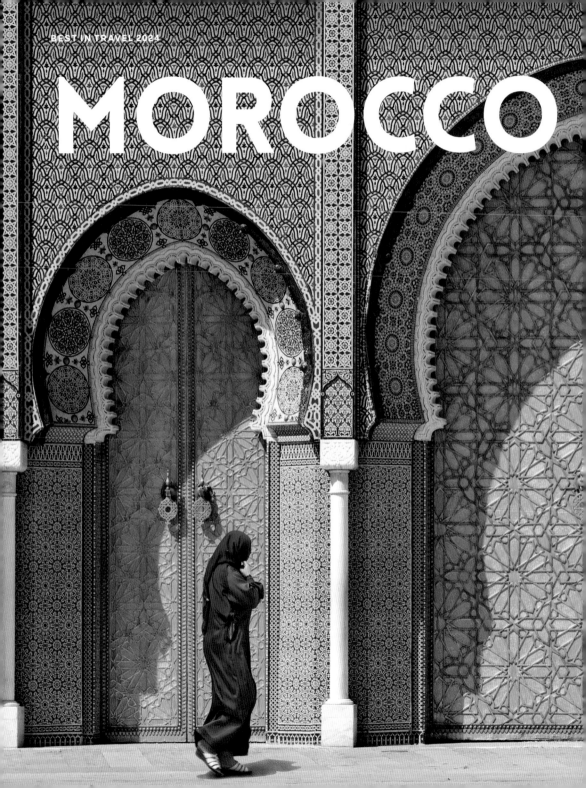

MOROCCO

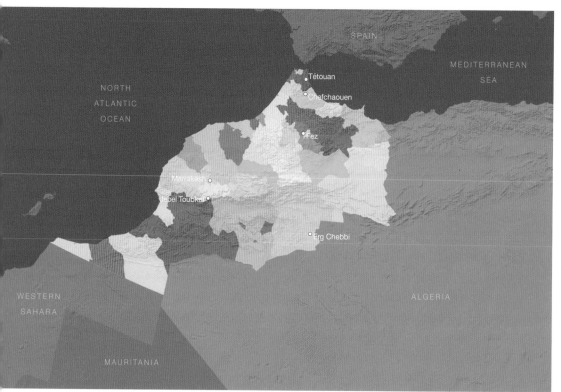

03

SPAIN

MEDITERRANEAN SEA

Tétouan

Chefchaouen

NORTH ATLANTIC OCEAN

Fez

Marrakesh

Jebel Toubkal

Erg Chebbi

WESTERN SAHARA

ALGERIA

MAURITANIA

There's nothing quite like wandering the Sahara Desert on camelback, hunting for bargains in a Marrakesh souq and exploring the enchanting blue city of Chefchaouen. But what makes Morocco stand out as a top destination for 2024? The North African country has made us cheer again thanks to the buzz from its historic performance at the World Cup, its ascension to the echelon of the world surf circuit, and its revived music festival, Mawazine, to start. Even if you've been before, 2024 is the time to (re)visit.

Ride the World Cup wave

The success of Morocco's Atlas Lions – the first African and Arab team to reach the semi-finals – was one of the most heartwarming stories of the 2022 FIFA World Cup, and the excitement hasn't worn off.

Morocco has made promising bids to host the 2030 FIFA World Cup and 2025 Africa Cup of Nations, and hosted the FIFA Club World Cup in 2022 for the third time in 10 years. In 2024, there's a great chance you'll get to see an Atlas Lions friendly against international opponents. If your trip doesn't align with one of those matches, Botola Pro, the competitive Moroccan league, is worth checking out, especially since it has a few players from the national team. Not a big football fan? It's still worth going to a game as the atmosphere is electric and fans love to synchronise with colourful tifo displays.

See you at sea

Morocco might inspire thoughts of desert dunes and dusty medinas, but don't be fooled – this is a beach country. With the seventh-longest coastline in Africa and access to both the Atlantic Ocean and Mediterranean Sea, Morocco is spoiled when it comes to seafront.

On the Atlantic Coast, Morocco has turned into a world-class surf destination. In 2022, the country hosted the first-ever pro surf competition on the continent, Surf Expo in Taghazout. Expect to see more competitions, but even if you aren't

Highlights

01 **Climb the tallest mountain** in North Africa, Jebel Toubkal in the High Atlas, in a seven-day loop to the 4167m (13,671ft) summit.

02 **Camel-trek** across the Erg Chebbi dunes in the Merzouga Desert and sleep out under the stars.

03 **Shop til you drop** for clothing, crafts and spices in the labyrinthine souqs of Marrakesh, Fez or Tetouan.

04 **Wander the blue-walled medina** alleys of Chefchaouen for a sky-tinted twist on a typical Moroccan streetscape.

27

Getting there

There are affordable flights from Europe and North America, but crossing the Strait of Gibraltar from Spain by ferry makes a great alternative. Once in Morocco, getting around has become easier thanks to the new high-speed train, Al Boraq, between Casablanca and Tangier.

When to go

The best time to visit Morocco is in the spring or autumn when the weather is neither too hot, nor snowy if you're planning to go trekking in the mountains.

Further reading

Before you go, read books by Laila Lalami and Paul Bowles.

a pro, Morocco is a great place for beginners and intermediates. In Essaouira, find prime surfing conditions as well as several coworking and coliving spaces for digital nomads.

Over on the Mediterranean Coast, the rail line to Tangier is due to be upgraded to a full high-speed link soon. The Beat Generation writers have left the city, but their old hangouts, like Cafe Hafa and Gran Cafe de Paris, remain. Out on the seafront, Tanja Marina Bay, opened in 2018, has given Tangier a shiny new face, with upmarket shopping, restaurants and even a dance club at the tip of the quay.

Fizzing festivals

After a three-year pause, Rabat's Mawazine Festival will make a triumphant comeback in 2024. The festival, which has previously been

> *Come try a bowl of snails fresh from the mountains. Snap a photo in our blue streets. Take a cooking class. Don't miss Chefchaouen, the kindest city in Morocco!*
>
> Chef Abdelghani Rhani, Chefchaouen

headlined by stars like Jennifer Lopez, Rihanna and David Guetta, is free for 90% of its acts, and attracts music-lovers by the millions.

For something more low-key, though no less enthralling, head to Marrakesh for the third edition of the International Storytelling Festival in February. It attracts storytellers from across the world who share their work and teach workshops over the week-long festival.

Other events to add to your 2024 calendar are Tafraoute's Almond Blossom Festival (February), M'hamid El Ghizlane's International Nomads Festival (March) and the Fez Festival of World Sacred Music (June). Keep in mind that Ramadan takes place from 10 March to 9 April, so if you go during that time, eating during daylight hours may not be possible.

1 Three of the seven golden doors fronting the Royal Palace of Fez **2** Tagine pots for sale in Chefchaouen **3** An extra-elaborate doorway in the 'Blue City' **4** Atlantic surf in Taghazout **5** Metro verve in Casablanca, Morocco's largest city **6** The alleyways of Tangier's medina provide an escape from the sun

CHILE

04

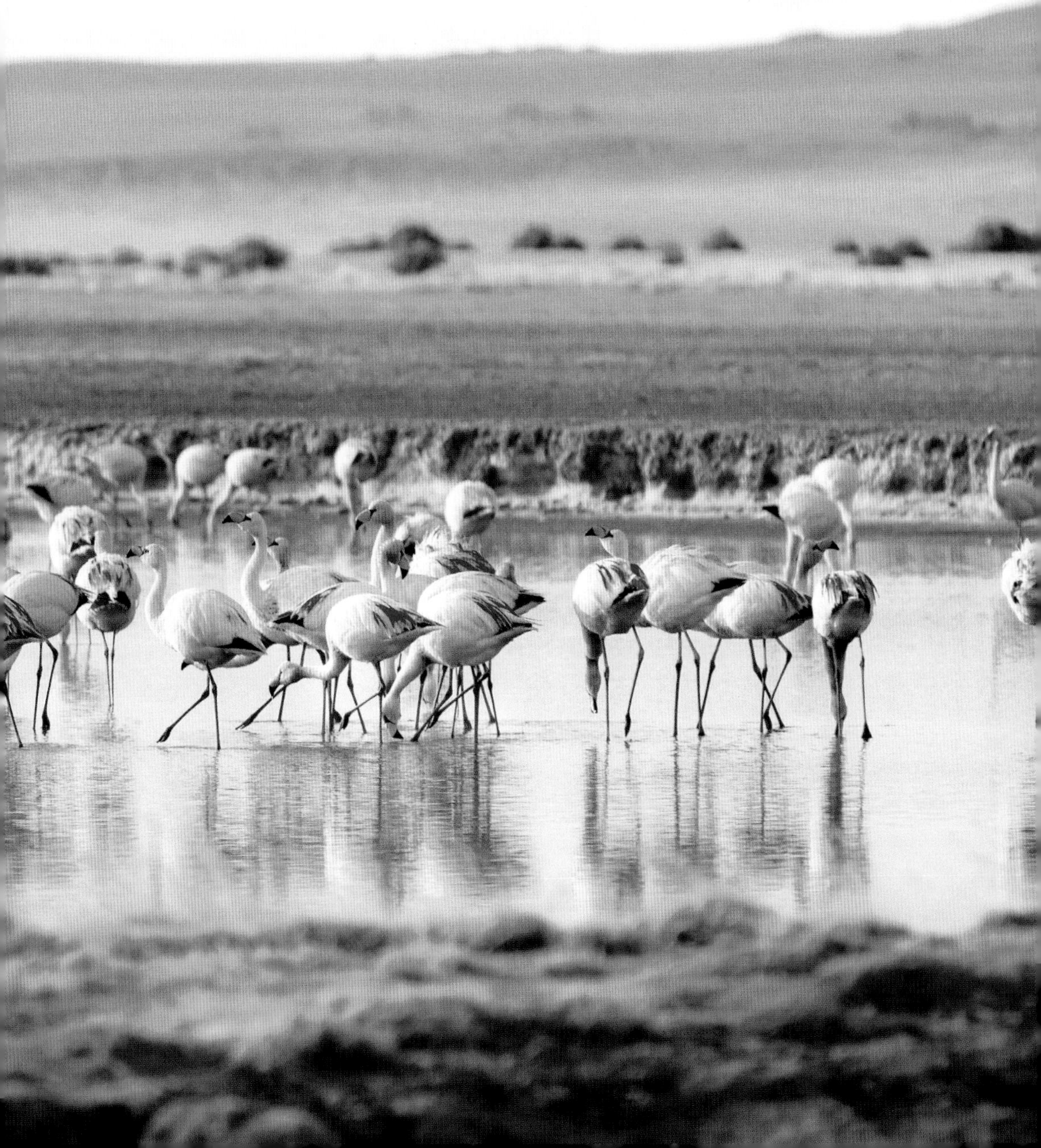

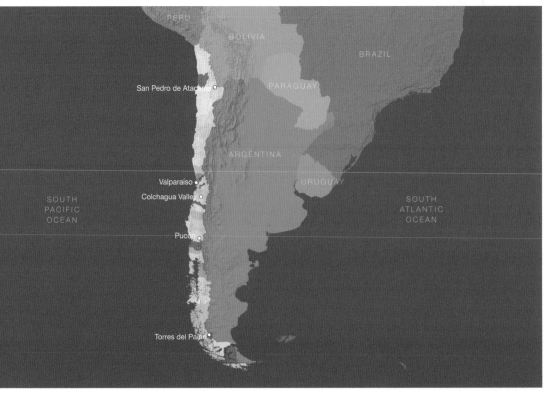

With expanded parklands, an ambitious new president and plans for a new equity-minded constitution, change permeates the air across Chile – a country of salt flats, rainforests, volcanoes, glaciers and fjords strung out along a 4720km (2650-mile) span. In the capital, Santiago, chefs are busy untapping the potential of endemic ingredients, while vintners in long-overlooked valleys find more natural ways to make their wines. Remote Rapa Nui (Easter Island) is reimagining its relationship with tourism for a more sustainable future, just as rewilding efforts in Patagonia are restoring the region's rich biodiversity.

Fire and ice

Chile is a land of wild extremes, and each one seems to be buzzing with new energy. In the Atacama, Earth's driest non-polar desert, the resort town of San Pedro lures travellers with its lunar-like valleys, remote archeological sites and blindingly white salt flats. Yet there are convincing reasons to head elsewhere in 2024, including a new museum near Arica, which will house the oldest mummies in the world. Down by the foggy fjords of Patagonia, Punta Arenas is now competing with its Argentine rival Ushuaia to become the main logistics hub for research and tourism to Antarctica, with more expedition ships departing from this southerly city than ever before. The remote Pacific territory of Rapa Nui has pivoted to a quality-over-quantity approach to tourism, with fewer flights and a higher park fee to encourage longer stays. Residents used their 868 days of pandemic isolation to beautify their streets, remove 10 tons of trash from the seabed, revive their Polynesian language, and plant more than a thousand vegetable gardens to make the island self-sustaining. Meanwhile, the vineyards of Mediterranean-like Middle Chile have undergone dramatic changes, too, with small producers in places such as the Itata and Maule valleys opening up to tourism and pivoting to low-intervention wines.

Plotting a greener future

Chile has gained more national parks over the past decade than just about anywhere else on Earth. Most have been along the Route of Parks

Highlights

01 **Hike the five-day W Trek** through Torres del Paine, enjoying the epic mountainscapes of Patagonia's preeminent park.

02 **Taste Chile's signature grape,** Carmenere, at the opulent wineries of the Colchagua Valley.

03 **Scramble up volcanoes** or across temperate rainforests before bathing in hot springs at Chile's adventure capital, Pucón.

04 **Get lost** in the steep and colourful alleyways of Valparaíso, the plucky port city covered in street art.

in the south, where places like Parque Nacional Patagonia are now at the forefront of a rewilding movement starring pumas, flightless ñandú (rheas) and endangered huemul deer. Yet, the two newest parks are in the north: Parque Nacional Desierto Florido (which protects a patch of the southern Atacama blanketed in flowers after heavy rains) and Parque Nacional Glaciares de Santiago, covering the glaciers above the capital.

A breath of fresh air in the capital

A social uprising against inequality that began in 2019 has led to major changes in Chile that are most apparent in greater Santiago, where 40% of all Chileans live. Two years of massive protests paved the way for reformer Gabriel Boric (one of the world's youngest leaders), who captured the zeitgeist fighting for environmental protections, Indigenous and LGBTQI+ rights and gender equality – all of which may be enshrined in a new constitution (drafted for a second time in 2023). Boric defied convention and moved into Santiago's working-class Barrio Yungay neighbourhood, whose heritage-listed buildings and graffiti-lined streets are suddenly in vogue.

The Central Andes are the highest mountains outside the Himalaya, so they are huge. People who might frequent the Alps or Rockies can come here and see these mountains that are actually a lot wilder.

Martín Le-Bert, director of Andes Santiago

In fact, some of the city's greatest new additions have popped up in traditionally underprivileged areas, including Pulpería Santa Elvira, a fabulous Chilean restaurant with haute cuisine takes on grandma-approved staples; and Factoría Franklin, an old industrial building now brimming with art galleries, gin distilleries and craft breweries. You can reach them on the city's ever-expanding metro system, or onboard the largest fleet of electric buses in the Americas. Meanwhile, the soaring Andes above town are the focus of a new campaign to turn Santiago into the 'world capital of mountain tourism' by 2030.

1 Flamingos feed at the Salar de Tara, near San Pedro de Atacama **2** Rapa Nui (Easter Island) moai **3** Barrio Yungay, Santiago **4** Puma in Torres del Paine National Park **5** Vines crisscross the Colchagua Valley wine region **6** Torres del Paine National Park

Getting there

Santiago International Airport has flights from cities in the Americas, Europe and Oceania.

When to go

There's no bad time to visit Chile, though its disparate regions shine in different seasons. Summer (January–March) is high season in Patagonia, the Lake District and coastal beach resorts, while skiers flock to the Andean slopes in winter (July–September), when the lower two-thirds of mainland Chile sees the most precipitation. Autumn means harvest celebrations in wine valleys, while spring is the greenest time of year for hiking in the central Andes. The Atacama Desert and Rapa Nui are year-round destinations with climates that vary little by month.

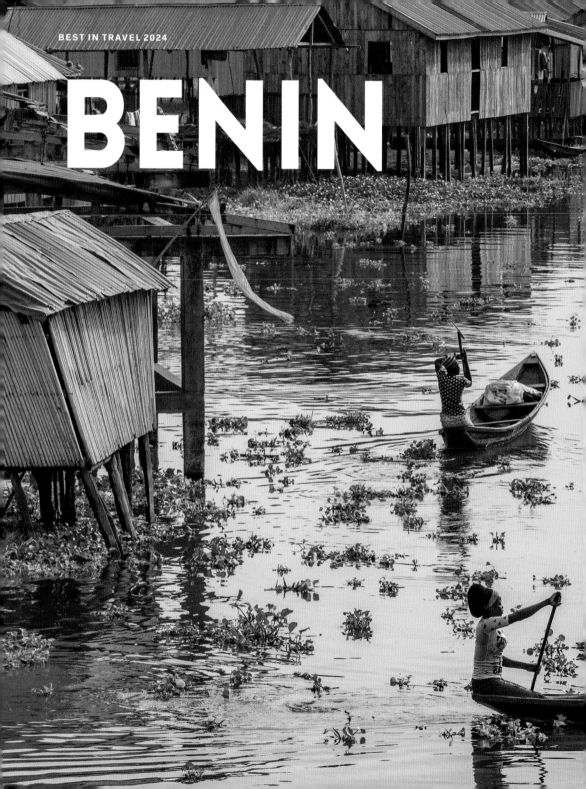

BENIN

05

Benin may be dwarfed by its neighbour to the east, Nigeria, but this bijou West African country punches above its weight in its charisma, history and cultural power. Once the site of the ancient Kingdom of Dahomey, it is also the spiritual home of voodoo, a fascinating and often misunderstood religion. Clued-in travellers are beating a path to Benin's palm-fringed beaches and some of the best national parks this side of the continent.

History on a mission

There's a lot of history to explore in Benin, from the Afro-Brazilian architectural heritage of Porto Novo to the Dahomey Mino, the famous all-woman Amazon warriors who

1 Catherina Unger/AWL Images © 2 anthony pappone/Getty Images ©

Highlights

01 **Join the spectacular** Ouidah Voodoo Festival on 10 January every year – a ceremonial riot of dancing, colours and fetishes.

02 **Witness human tenacity** in Ganvié village, the 'Venice of Africa', built out on stilts in Lake Nokoué.

03 **Roam the savannah** with some of West Africa's best wildlife in Parc National de la Pendjari: lions, elephants, cheetahs and leopards.

04 **Get to the heart** of the powerful Kingdom of Dahomey at Abomey, once home to iconic female warriors.

3 Eric Lafforgue/Art in All of Us/Getty Images ©

have long fascinated outsiders. This interest has snowballed since *The Woman King* was released in 2022. Its celluloid depiction of the iconic female fighters is bringing new and appreciative crowds to the museum at Abomey's Royal Palaces, a Unesco World Heritage site. As part of its mission to reclaim its historical artefacts, Benin is set to become West Africa's top destination for art and culture with the planned opening of the Museum of the Epic of the Amazons and Kings of Dahomey in the next couple of years. Located in the Royal Palaces, it will retell the grandeur of the Dahomey Empire and display 26 works of art returned by France, and 350 art objects.

Culture for the ages

Benin's art scene has flourished ever since Cotonou's Fondation Zinsou became one of the first African contemporary art museums to open in sub-Saharan Africa (there's now a site in Ouidah, too). The country will be showcasing its talent to the wider world in 2024, when it gets its first ever national pavilion at the Venice Biennale.

1 Canoes are the conveyance of choice in Ganvié **2** A traditional village of the Taneka people, in the Atakora Mountains of the north **3** Porto Novo's Great Mosque **4** Hands-free market trading in the city of Abomey **5** The Étoile Rouge roundabout in Cotonou, Benin's largest city **6** A masked Egungun dancer

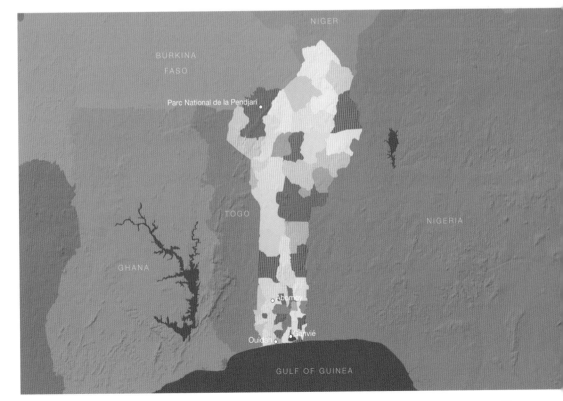

We love Benin's ease of access, its rich cultural heritage, beautiful beaches, and, above all, the clever mix of tradition and modernity. There's a feeling that everything is possible.

Stéphane Brabant and Armelle Adjovi, Afrikafun, MSK Concept and FIWÊ travel app

But it's not just contemporary culture that attracts international visitors to Benin – the country's ancient traditions are a big draw, especially voodoo, an animist belief system that is more complex than its frequent cartoon treatment. Its rituals are celebrated in January each year during the Voodoo Festival in the historic city of Ouidah, just inland from the western coast. Voodoo's influence can still be seen across the Atlantic in Afro-Brazilian, Haitian and Cuban cultures, where elements of it are practised by descendants of enslaved people, many of whom were taken from these shores. No trip to Benin would be complete without a visit to Ouidah's beach, where the Gate of No Return marks the spot where enslaved Africans were forced to board ships for the New World. The beaches are now a place of pilgrimage for Diasporan Africans who come here for sober reflection on this devastating chapter in history.

All-natural appeal

Benin has an impressive variety of landscapes, from palm-fringed Atlantic beaches to the rugged savannah of the north. The Parc National de la Pendjari is enjoying a successful reboot

thanks to government conservation efforts, making it a top wildlife reserve in West Africa – a region that's lost much of its Big Five species – that vies with the more famous parks of East and Southern Africa. Sightings of elephants, buffalo and lions are almost guaranteed in Pendjari, and if you're lucky you might even spot cheetahs and leopards. (Before planning a visit, check the security situation on the border of Burkina Faso.) For water-borne excursions there's Ganvié stilt village, and pirogue rides along the Black River as it cuts a water-lilied swathe through Adjarra village just outside the capital city, Porto Novo.

Wherever you go in Benin, you'll find genial people, good roads and hotels, and restaurants that throb to Afrobeat rhythms. We suggest you go there now before the rest of the world fully wakes up to its appeal.

Getting there

There are direct flights to Cotonou from Belgium, France and several African countries.

When to go

Benin has two very distinct seasons – the wet and the dry. Wet season is slightly cooler (though still hot) and lasts from around May/June to September, with heavy but short downpours. The best time to visit is in the dry season, which runs from November to February. The Voodoo Festival takes place every 10 January.

Further reading

For good historical fiction read *Thread of Gold Beads* by Nike Campbell-Fatoki, and *The Viceroy of Ouidah* by Bruce Chatwin.

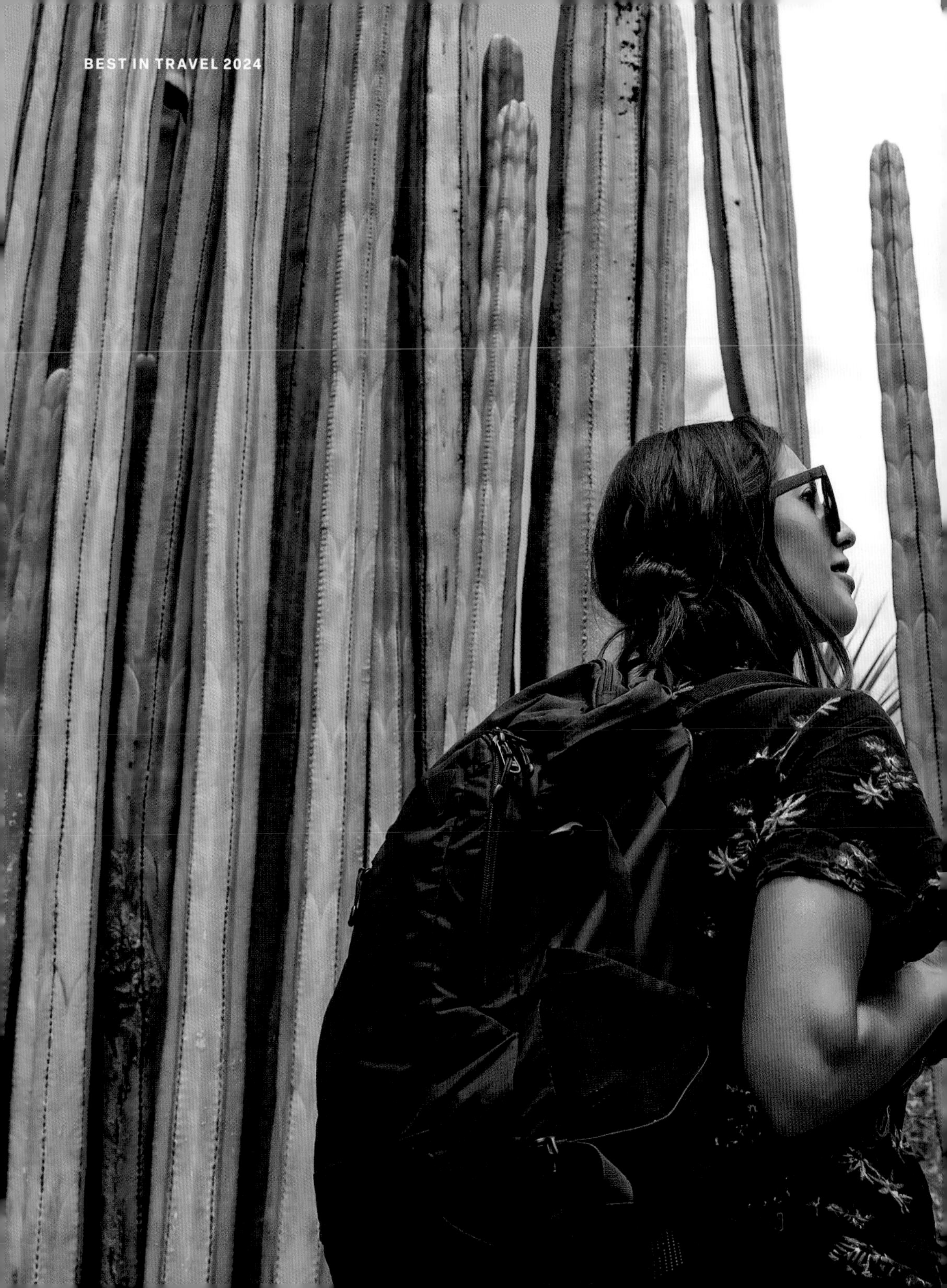

06

MEXICO

What do a shiny new railway, an epic stargazing event and a nascent superhighway to the coast have in common? All offer truly compelling reasons to visit Mexico this year. And each has a unique appeal. A journey aboard a freshly launched train bound for Caribbean beaches and ancient Maya ruins. A life-affirming solar eclipse viewed from the golden sands of Mazatlán. Or a road trip to bohemian beach towns along Oaxaca's ruggedly beautiful coast.

Riding the Maya Train

Imagine rattling along an intercity railway that snakes its way to astonishing Maya ruins and mesmerising turquoise beaches. Forging a

1 Bisual Studio/Stocksy United © 2 Thomas Barwick/Getty Images ©

Highlights

01 **View a glorious solar eclipse** in Old Mazatlán, then drop by El Presidio for fresh seafood in the atmospheric historic centre.

02 **Dramatically situated Maya ruins** and nearby cenotes (swimmable sinkholes) deliver serious wow factor in Tulum.

03 **The hilltop infinity pool** and ocean-view rooms at Casa Kalmar will have you thinking Zipolite is the best place in the world.

04 **Hop aboard the Maya Train** to explore mysterious Maya ruins in Palenque, rising up from a misty jungle home to howler monkeys.

3 Kelli Hayden/Shutterstock ©

1525km (948-mile) loop route in southeastern Mexico, the new Tren Maya (Maya Train) is set to dramatically transform travel in the Yucatán Peninsula, a region also known for its savoury cuisine and rich indigenous culture. A Maya Train itinerary might go something like this: start with wondrous Maya ruins in Chichén Itzá, hop off for reef diving in Puerto Morelos, then cap things off in a hip Tulum beach bar. The train also stops at Cancún airport, the peninsula's main point of entry. The railway has already created thousands of jobs, and the government megaproject aims to bring tourism to lesser-known communities, but environmentalists have concerns that the heavy trains might collapse a delicate underground network of rivers and limestone pools, known as cenotes. Sustainability and overtourism loom large in the years ahead.

Total eclipse

Even if you're not much of an astronomy buff, any time you can experience someplace new during an awe-inspiring celestial event like a total solar eclipse, it takes on a larger-than-life quality. Around noon on April 8, 2024, Mazatlán will be in the path of totality, meaning stargazers can plop down on their favourite beach, put on those funny viewing glasses and watch the Pacific coast resort city go dark for an impressive four-plus minutes. To appreciate the spectacle away from the

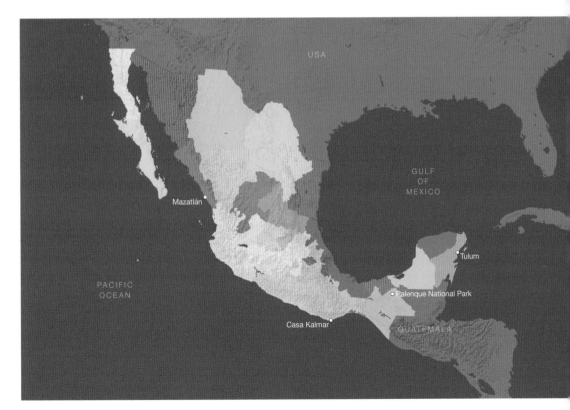

4 Justin Foulkes/Lonely Planet © 5 Karen Doody/Stocktrek Images/Getty Images © 6 Bisual Photo/Shutterstock ©

Zipolite will swoop you up and reignite your mojo. Spending time here, you're destined to be inspired, create something and witness spectacular art and performance. It's the true home of the free.

April Shannon, owner of jewellery workshop Taller la Joya in Zipolite, Oaxaca

hubbub of downtown, head to the palm-fringed Isla de la Piedra and soak up the scenery over drinks in a low-key *palapa*-thatched bar. To behold even more natural wonders in Mazatlán, hook up an excursion with Onca Explorations, an ecotourism outfit that makes nature conservation a focal point. Onca runs responsible whale-watching outings from December to April and wild dolphin and birding trips year-round.

Cool beach vibes
A new expressway connecting Oaxaca City and Puerto Escondido will zip you to the beach in just three hours, making it a cinch to reach the splendid southern coast. After hanging with the surfer crowd in Puerto Escondido, home to the 'Mexican Pipeline', head southeast for Zipolite, a blissed-out hippie enclave famous for its clothing-optional beach, LGBTQI+-friendly accommodation and unabashed, anything-goes vibe. Most of the action centres around the

long beach and Avenida Roca Blanca, a low-rise strip of seafood restaurants, open-air bars and intentionally rustic hotels. If beach-bumming gets old, check out the colourful woodcrafts made at Piña Palmera, a rehabilitation centre for people with disabilities. Then swing by Zircolite, a welcoming circus school that teaches acrobatics, fire juggling and African dancing, all useful skills for Zipolite's beach bashes. Nearby sister town Mazunte exudes a similar freewheeling air.

1 Giant cacti in the Jardín Etnobotánico, Oaxaca
2 Tacos are a national snack 3 San Martín Tilcajete village is famed for its artisan-crafted carvings
4 Entertainment in Oaxaca's Mercado Benito Juárez
5 Cenote diving on the Riviera Maya 6 The ancient Zapotec city of Monte Albán

Getting there

Cancún and Mexico City are the busiest international airports, but most big cities have direct flights from major US hubs.

When to go

A visit in January or February means dry and relatively cooler climes, providing some relief in humid coastal destinations. It's also whale-watching season along the Pacific coast. In Mazatlán, February is carnival time.

Further reading

Read Bernal Díaz del Castillo's fascinating firsthand account of a conquistador foot soldier in *The Conquest of New Spain*, or Nobel prize-winner Octavio Paz's *The Labyrinth of Solitude* for insights into Mexican identity.

UZBEKISTAN

From oasis to oasis across Uzbekistan, over the sands of the Kyzylkum and Karakum deserts, modern tourists follow the trading networks of centuries past. Though high-speed rail and a convenient domestic flight network have replaced the camel caravans that once crossed between prosperous fortress towns, the ancient cultural hubs of Samarkand, Bukhara and Khiva still evoke the era of the Silk Road. To the north, in the Nuratau Mountains, a community-based tourism initiative hosts visitors hoping to slow into a more local pace of life with shepherding communities living beneath ruined strongholds.

1 monticello/Shutterstock © 2 NICOLA MESSANA PHOTOS/Shutterstock ©

Highlights

01 **Stand dwarfed** beneath the immense *medressahs* of the Registan in Samarkand, once the heart of the Timurid Empire.

02 **Sip tea** with Bukhara's elders in the teahouses of Lyabi Hauz or strike a deal with shopkeepers in the covered bazaars.

03 **Ascend the heights** of Khiva's Islam Khodja Minaret for stunning views across the Ichon-Qala fortress to the deserts beyond.

04 **Hike in the** little-visited Nuratau Mountains, exploring old shepherd trails and enjoying family homestay dinners.

3 angela Meier/Shutterstock ©

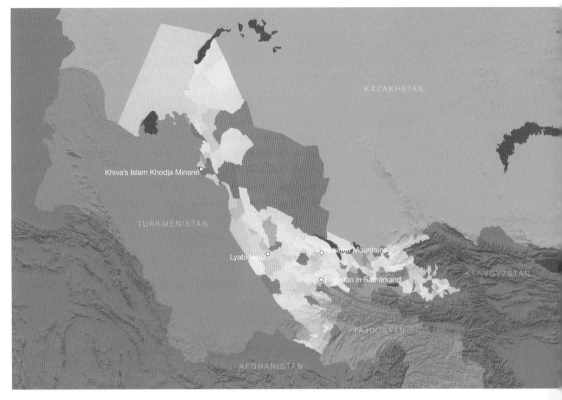

Silk Road cities

From Chinese silks and Iranian dates, to the armies of merchants that moved them, Uzbekistan's Silk Road cities have been Central Asia's cultural and commercial hubs for thousands of years. From the 4th century BCE onwards, the oasis towns of Samarkand, Bukhara and Khiva thrived as medieval empires built on tribute, trade and spoils of war to become dominant powers in middle Asia, remaining independent emirates until subsumption into the Russian Empire in the late 19th century.

Uzbekistan's three great Silk Road cities each retain a unique character, and all remain easily reached by rail or flight directly from the capital city, Tashkent. Samarkand is defined by the central Registan square and three imposing *medressah* religious schools that surround it – though don't miss the splendid mosaics of the Gūr-i Amīr tomb of Timur, founder of the Timurid Empire, which reached from modern Turkey to India; and the even more dazzling Shah-i-Zinda necropolis of his relatives and advisers.

Bukhara integrates history into modern life more directly. From the central Lyabi Hauz square's pools, medieval streets radiate out through residential neighbourhoods interspersed with mosques, *medressahs* and popular covered trading halls – each once dedicated to a specific craft (currency changers, hat makers, jewellers and carpets) but now full of souvenir vendors; while the wares may have changed, both the

After Samarkand, see the real village life. I suggest visiting Ohalik, a village located close to hiking trails where you'll meet villagers and visit their traditional stone houses.

Abdu Samadov, Samarkand-based tour guide

spirit of commerce and international clientele continue to draw upon Silk Road traditions.

Remotest of the three, small Khiva's well-preserved Ichon-Qala Old Town and fortress has only recently begun drawing tourists in numbers to match its better-known Silk Road siblings. Often described as an open-air museum, both for sheer scale and for level of preservation, Khiva was named the Tourism Capital of the Islamic World for 2024. Concurrent with a planned finalisation of high-speed rail lines from Bukhara, it can expect to see visitors coming in greater numbers than ever.

Traditional lifestyles and ancient fortresses

Off the old trading routes, away from prying eyes, small mountain communities long remained hidden in the low valleys of the Nuratau Mountains. To the north of the great Silk Road towns, nearly every small village is protected by an abandoned fortress, now crumbling back into the cliffs, though the shepherd paths that connect the villages still see use by villagers and tourists.

Though the inhabitants of Nuratau's small villages were collectivised during the Soviet era, independence saw a return to older ways, and as Uzbekistan's government continues to liberalise

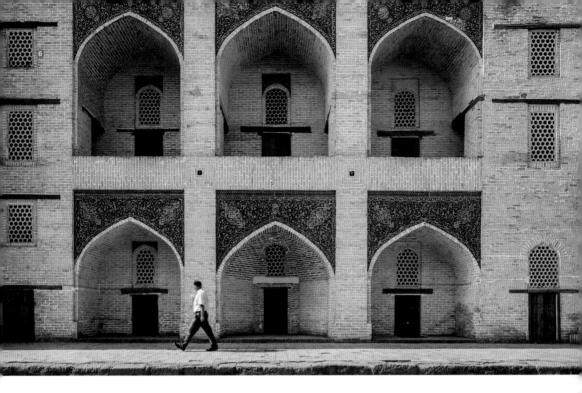

since a 2016 change of leadership, the ease of opening small business has seen a burst of family guesthouses open to welcome walkers who day-hike from village to village, exploring the area.

Regardless of where an Uzbekistan itinerary leads, getting into the country is certainly easier today than the caravaners had it. Citizens of more than 80 countries (including the UK and all of the EU) can enter Uzbekistan visa-free for at least 30 days, and 75 countries that require visas (including the United States) can apply through a simplified e-Visa regime.

1 The Registan is Samarkand's centrepiece square
2 The city's more intimate Shah-i-Zinda tombs are also World Heritage-listed 3 Rural escape in the Nuratau Mountains 4 Dining outside at Bukhara's Lyabi Hauz 5 Fresh bread in Tashkent's Chorsu Bazaar 6 Bukhara is a quintessential Silk Road city

Getting there

Most visitors fly into the capital city Tashkent or smaller Samarkand airport, though some intrepid travellers still enter overland on longer Silk Road journeys from Kazakhstan, Kyrgyzstan or Tajikistan.

When to go

The best seasons to visit Uzbekistan, April to May and September to October, are also the busiest. Consider an off-season winter visit when crowds are few and temperatures are chilly but still manageable.

Further reading

Delve into *The Devil's Dance* by Hamid Ismailov; Peter Hopkirk's *The Great Game*; and *Shadow of the Silk Road* by Colin Thubron.

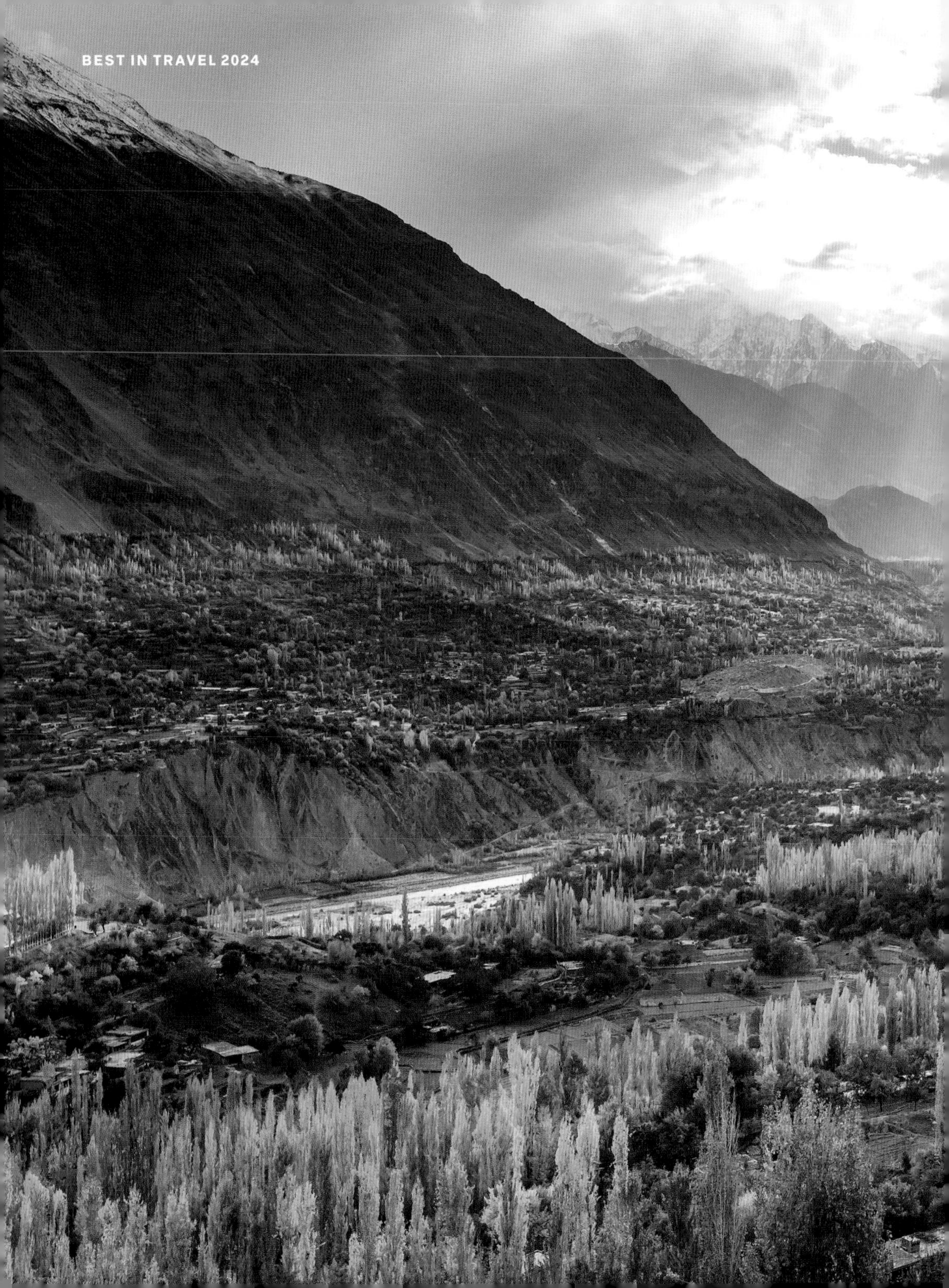

08

PAKISTAN

For years, Pakistan has **been overlooked by mainstream tourism,** but hardy adventurers have kept the travel flame alive, ready for the day when Pakistan rises to reclaim its rightful place in the top tier of travel destinations. That day could be close – with easing political tensions, adventure tour companies are returning to Pakistan's buzzing bazaars, Mughal-built mosques, alpine valleys and snow-dusted Himalayan passes. There's an ethical incentive too – every rupee you spend in Pakistan will help the country rebuild after the devastating floods of 2022.

Asia's biggest travel secret

Pakistan's thorny politics attract more press attention than its abundant wonders, but many

Highlights

01 **Getting lost in Lahore** – the capital of Punjab is a tangled maze of Mughal-built bazaars, awash with mosques and magic.

02 **Driving the Karakoram Highway** – the breathless road linking Pakistan and China cuts a transect through the high Himalaya.

03 **Mountain encounters** in Hunza and Skardu – high-altitude valleys serve up some of the most beautiful views on the planet.

04 **Hike the Fairy Meadows** – the trek to the mountaineers' base camp for Nanga Parbat is a journey steeped in silence and serenity.

travellers rate the Islamic Republic as one of their favourite destinations in Asia. Certainly, there are few places in the world where the past feels so close at hand – we defy anyone to wander through Lahore's Mughal-built markets or the time-frayed fortresses of Hunza and Skardu and not feel transported back several centuries.

But, we do concede that Pakistan is one of the world's more challenging travel destinations. The security situation must be navigated carefully, with an ever-changing map of areas that are off-limits, and infrastructure may be patchy away from the big, built-up cities. On the flipside, you're guaranteed a 100% authentic experience – tourist enclaves are almost non-existent, and every stop in Pakistan is steeped in the colours and flavours of the subcontinent.

Adventurers who make the trip can expect unforgettable experiences. Hikers and mountaineers go weak at the knees at the mention of the alpine meadows around 8126m (26,660ft) Nanga Parbat. Travellers who value scenery over comfort wax lyrical about the magnificent 1300km (808 miles) of the Karakoram Highway, linking Pakistan to China via the parched, high-altitude valleys of Gilgit-

1 Autumn hues in the Hunza Valley 2 Driving the Karakoram Highway 3 Lost in Lahore's backstreets 4 The peach harvest is crucial to Northern Pakistan 5 Backstage at Fashion Pakistan Week in Karachi 6 Nanga Parbat viewed from the Fairy Meadows in Gilgit-Baltistan

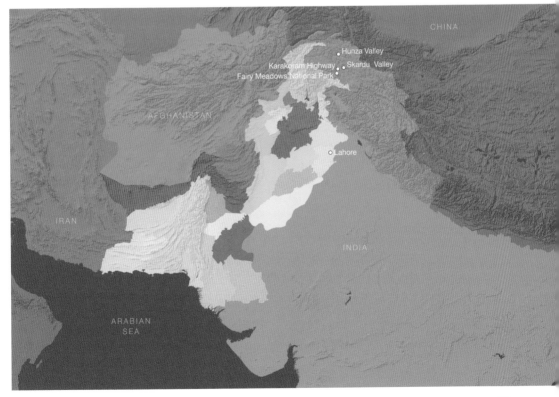

The people of Gilgit-Baltistan are known for their hospitality and friendliness. I was born and raised here, and I love the fresh air and stunning natural scenery, from high mountain peaks to glaciers, lakes and rivers.

Shahid Hussain, director of adventure tour company, Trango Adventure

Baltistan. If living history is more your thing, simply step back through the ages in the timeless bazaars of Lahore, Rawalpindi and Karachi.

Turning a corner

Tourism to Pakistan has had its ups and downs. During the heyday of overland travel, Peshawar and Lahore were essential stops on the hippie trail from Europe to India, but geopolitics became a major obstacle to travel. Russian and American entanglements in Afghanistan put Pakistan at the epicentre of the Cold War and the War on Terror, and conflict with India over the status of Kashmir has rumbled on for more than 75 years.

But much of Pakistan still lies within reach. Thronging cities such as Lahore, Karachi, Islamabad and Rawalpindi promise full-colour cultural encounters, and the northern section of the Karakoram Highway serves up endless miles of travel through some of the most humbling landscapes on Earth.

More importantly, with improvements to the security situation, adventure travel agencies such as Intrepid and Exodus are returning, offering an easy-in for travellers seeking extra support in this complicated country. Simultaneously, investment from China is improving infrastructure along the old Silk Road route, meaning easier overlanding through Pakistan's mountainous north.

Visiting now is also an opportunity to help Pakistan bounce back from one of its worst-ever natural disasters, following the catastrophic climate-change-linked floods of 2022. Those who come will discover a country that defies expectations: listen to the pilgrims chanting Qawwāli devotional songs at ancient Sufi shrines such as Lahore's Data Darbar, or wander the still and silent Fairy Meadows near Nanga Parbat, and you'll quickly understand why locals describe Pakistan as the land of peace.

Getting there

Karachi, Lahore and Islamabad are the main international gateways, with flights to Middle Eastern hubs and select European cities. Coming by land, consider the Karakoram Highway from Kashgar in China.

When to go

May to October is the main travel window, but the south is affected by monsoon rains from June to August; escape downpours in dry, mountainous Gilgit-Baltistan.

Further reading

Must-reads include *A Case of Exploding Mangoes* by Mohammed Hanif; *In Other Rooms, Other Wonders* by Daniyal Mueenuddin; and *Shame* by Salman Rushdie.

CROATIA

09

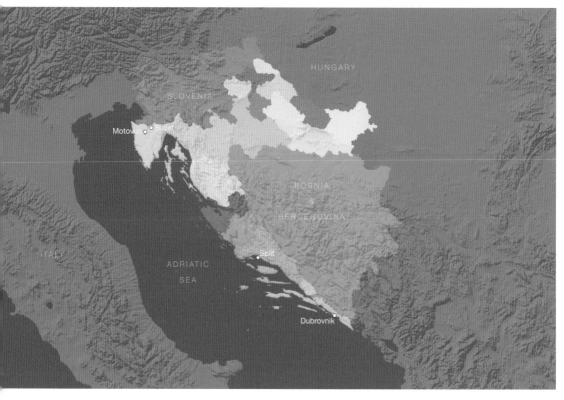

HUNGARY

SLOVENIA

Motovun ○ ○ Buzet

BOSNIA
&
HERCEGOVINA

ITALY

ADRIATIC
SEA

Split ○

Dubrovnik ○

With its sun-kissed coastline, myriad islands, dramatic mountains and historic walled cities, Croatia is no stranger to best-destination lists. Travel to this tourism hot spot has become even easier recently, with its entry into both the border-free Schengen Area and the Eurozone. Now you can journey overland all the way from Lisbon to Dubrovnik without once having to hand over a passport or change currency. If you were looking for an excuse to cross Croatia off your bucket list, it's easier to do it in 2024 than ever before.

1 canadastock/Shutterstock © 2 Laura Edwards/Lonely Planet ©

Trans-Europe express

Croatia's gorgeous Adriatic coast is its most celebrated feature, along with its 1200-plus islands and islets. Wherever you are, the backdrop is inevitably extraordinary – whether it's an ancient town behind sturdy walls, or the craggy limestone peaks of the mountain ranges that stretch all the way along the coast.

Some things haven't changed, such as the simple joy of lazing in the sun beside crystal-clear waters, occasionally shifting from your deckchair to order another glass of chilled Dalmatian wine. What is different is that when you're ordering that wine, you no longer have to calculate a tricky conversion from the old currency (*hrvatska kuna*), as Croatia, after 10 years in the European Union, has finally adopted the euro.

Likewise, the old days of presenting passports at dual border stations to enter the country from EU neighbours Slovenia and Hungary are gone, speeding up journeys considerably. Also consigned to history is the need to pass in and out of Bosnia when travelling between Split and Dubrovnik, thanks to the opening of the Pelješac Bridge and the completion of a new highway.

Peninsula perks

The striking 2.4km (1.5 mile) multi-span cable-stayed Pelješac Bridge has shone a spotlight onto a previously overlooked part of the Croatian coastline, the Pelješac Peninsula. Less than 50km (30 miles) from the famously beautiful walled city of Dubrovnik, this mountainous finger of land has its own striking 14th-century fortifications in

Highlights

01 **Croatia has dozens of walled towns**, but Dubrovnik is the most striking, with honey-coloured fortifications rising above cerulean waters.

02 **Discover Split's** remarkably well-preserved Ancient Roman palace, at the core of this major city of the coast.

03 **Make use of** the extensive ferry network along the coast to explore some of Croatia's many idyllic islands.

04 **If your culinary fantasies** include eating truffles multiple times a day, follow your nose north to Motovun and Buzet in Istria.

4

Getting there

Croatia has eight international airports, the most useful of which are Zagreb, Split and Dubrovnik. It's also connected to the European train network, and ferries shunt backwards and forwards from Italy.

When to go

The absolute peak season is July and August; aim for the two months on either side for less-crowded beaches.

Further reading

Marcus Tanner's *Croatia: A Nation Forged In War* is a good introduction to the country's troubled history. For a witty collection of essays, try Slavenka Drakulić's *Café Europa: Life After Communism*.

the shape of the 5.5km (3.5 miles) of defensive walls linking Ston with Mali Ston ('Little Ston') over the hill. The conjoined towns are known for their large flat oysters, harvested here since Roman times, and a surprisingly delicious spiced pasta cake, *Stonska torta*.

Nearby Prapatno has one of Croatia's finest sandy beaches, while – further along the peninsula – the sun-blasted slopes of Dingač and Postup produce Croatia's premier red wine. The peninsula is also the gateway to the intriguing islands of Mljet and Korčula, home to still more beaches, Roman ruins, walled towns and a national park.

The beauty within

While the coast may get all the attention, there's plenty to see inland as well. In the coastal hinterland, the lake-filled national parks of Krka

The Vis archipelago has some of the most extraordinary coastline in the entire Adriatic, with so much diversity that it's recently been recognised as a Unesco Geopark.

Zoran Milosavljević, fisherman and day-excursion skipper.

and Plitvice Lakes are almost preternaturally beautiful. If you weren't witnessing them with your own eyes, you'd swear that someone had applied a digital filter to achieve those dazzling shades of blue and green.

The interior of Istria, Croatia's northernmost peninsula, is dotted with picturesque hilltop towns overlooking the vineyards, olive groves and truffle-secluding old forests that have made the region a culinary highlight. Further inland, the nation's capital Zagreb brims with Central European charm, revelling in a vibrant coffee culture and excellent museums and art galleries.

Continue on to the bucolic farmland of the Zagorje, Međimurje and Slavonia regions and a more rustic side of Croatia comes into view. The country may be small but there's plenty of diversity for adventurous travellers to uncover.

1 Dubrovnik and its cable car 2 Folk dress in the coastal town of Primošten 3 Kayaking the blue waters near Dubrovnik 4 The new Pelješac Bridge means borderless drives the length of Croatia 5 Zagreb's Old Town has a more Central European than Mediterranean look 6 Istria's truffle bounty

ST LUCIA

10

Sunswept beaches, powdery white sand and cerulean-tinged waters are accurate descriptors for the island with an iron grip on the World's Best Honeymoon Destination designation. But recently, St Lucian tourism officials have consciously shifted toward authentic, local culture that centres the island's strong heritage, distinctive traditions and creative proclivities. This renewed focus also includes St Lucian cuisine, which is a mélange of African, East Indian and European (British and French) influences. This immersive experience is ideal for Carib-ophiles searching for something beyond the typical all-inclusive stay in 2024.

1 Paul Baggaley/Getty Images © 2 Orietta Gaspari/Getty Images ©

Highlights

01 **The best ice cream** in St Lucia can be found at Au Poye Park on the Charles family estate in Fond Gens Libre.

02 **It's an unofficial tradition** to pick up some creole loaves loaded with cheese or luncheon meat from Thomazo Local Bread, a roadside bakery, when driving through Dennery.

03 **The colourful beachfront** oasis of Irie Bar in Gros-Islet village, at the northern tip of the island, is a laidback respite offering cold drinks, flavourful food and pure vibes.

3 WireImage/Getty Images ©

A return to form

If there's one thing St Lucians love, it's a 'bon tan' (good time) and a 'lime' (hang out). The fête scene had been in a pandemic-induced lull for the past three years, but the extended hiatus has finally ended, starting with the return of arguably the best international music festival in the Caribbean: the Saint Lucia Jazz and Arts Festival. Staying committed to honouring the island's heritage, the festival includes an art component featuring local dance, theatre and cuisine. With a lineup boasting 17-time Grammy winner Sting, reggae legend Buju Banton and gospel royalty CeCe Winans, musicophiles will want to book early for what promises to be an impressive 2024 slate.

After this May event, there's soon another big-hitting festival as St Lucia enters what's otherwise its visitor low-season. Carnival in July is also back, with the vibrant pageantry and spectacle only growing in pomp and splendour. The weeks leading up to the colourful conclusion include a steady stream of fringe events, from

1 The twin peaks of the Pitons are the standout symbol of St Lucia **2** The colourful west-coast village of Canaries **3** Soca artist Alison Hinds performing at the Saint Lucia Jazz and Arts Festival **4** It's always time for chocolate **5** The forested interior makes for fabulous ziplining **6** Caribbean blue in Canaries Bay

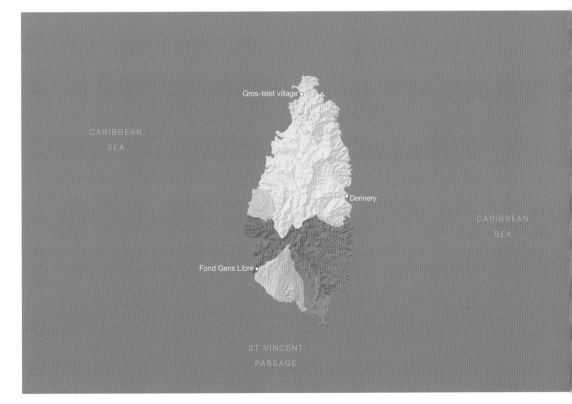

The sun shines differently in St Lucia. It's the perfect climate for relaxing and rejuvenating. I love the warmth of the people and how everyone and everything is connected, so there's a close network for finding things.

Nesa Constantine-Beaubrun, Castries-born business owner

boat rides to breakfast fêtes and 'wet' parties. But the pièce de résistance comes with the flood of bejewelled and feathered revellers chipping down the parade route undergirded by a heavy soca bassline.

A local renaissance

St Lucia's chocolate-producing past dates back to the 1700s when the island exported cocoa beans to Europe and North America to produce rich, flavourful premium chocolate. Local cocoa was considered among the finest in the world, grown in nutrient-dense volcanic soil in temperate conditions. The island returns to its roots with Cacoa Sainte Lucie, a premier agro-processing company turning out micro-batches of decadent gourmet chocolate in Belvedere, Canaries. At the helm is Canaries village resident Maria Jackson, a former pastry chef and St Lucia's first female chocolatier. Cacoa Sainte Lucie has expanded to include intimate demonstrations, hands-on tutorials and a recently opened restaurant

featuring chocolate-infused fare, like cocoa-crusted grilled mahi-mahi.

Nearby, in Anse La Verdure, Plas Kassav (Kwéyol for Cassava Place) is a family-run roadside bakery centred around another historically significant crop. The galvanised hut-turned-mini-factory has been a community staple since 1998, save for a fire in 2017 that levelled the business to the ground. Since the rebuild, the bakery continues to offer guided tours to walk visitors through the process of grating raw cassava, extracting the liquid and parching the pulp in large copper cauldrons. The resulting flour forms the base of the densely packed and unleavened cassava bread infused with uniquely Lucian flavours of coconut, cherry and raisin, apple and raisin, cinnamon, banana, chocolate, saltfish, smoked herring, ginger, pineapple, apricot and peanut.

Getting there
St Lucia has two airports – Hewanorra (UVF) and George FL Charles Airport (SLU) – welcoming direct flights from North America, Europe and other Caribbean islands.

When to go
There's hardly a wrong time to visit the Caribbean. The island does have a rainy season from June to November – a period that also sees the most risk of hurricanes – however the scattered showers are typically not prolonged enough to derail an entire trip.

Further reading
For some background before visiting, *A History of St Lucia* by Jolien Harmsen and others is the most definitive work.

LONELY PLANET'S

BEST IN TRAVEL 2024
TOP 10 CITIES

Nairobi, Kenya / Paris, France / Montréal, Canada / Mostar, Bosnia and Hercegovina / Philadelphia, Pennsylvania / Manaus, Brazil / Jakarta, Indonesia / Prague, Czech Republic / İzmir, Turkey / Kansas City, USA

NAIROBI, KENYA

01

Long underestimated by travellers and even by its own residents, Kenya's capital is finally staking its claim as a global centre of culture. No one is suggesting that Nairobi is for the fainthearted, but if you look past the gruff exterior, it's sizzling with unmissable travel experiences. The city is shrugging off the colonial gaze and embracing its unique rhythms, with an impressive array of restaurants inspired by local cuisine, and a steady rotation of arts and cultural venues that has given rise to a distinct kind of Nairobi cool.

Culinary glow-up

Nairobi's food scene is growing and glowing up. International menus dominate, offering an

1 drewcar85/Shutterstock © 2 Ariel Moscardi/Courtesy of Cultiva ©

Highlights

01 **Watch a performance** of traditional music and dance at the Bomas of Kenya for a lightning-fast tour of the country.

02 **Walk through** the Ngong Hills Forest at sunrise for views of Mt Kenya and Mt Kilimanjaro on a clear day.

03 **Visit the Nairobi National Park** for a safari on a budget with the city's evolving skyline as a backdrop.

04 **Climb to the top** of the Kenyatta International Conference Centre for a 360-degree view of the city. (There's also a lift!)

3 Giulia Lorenzon/Unsplash ©

eclectic mix of food from the many cultures that have crossed paths through the city over the decades. But locals demanded, restaurants listened, and today an impressive array of eateries are experimenting with local ingredients and cuisines, challenging chefs to keep it interesting with what's available. All budgets are served, with Cultiva in Karen, nestled within the garden where many of the ingredients are grown, a top pick for deep pockets with its ever-changing menu of hot food and baked treats. Budget-conscious travellers should consider the nine-course tasting menu at Amaica in Peponi, or Kienyeji's in Kilimani, which specialises in cuisine from western Kenya including ox tongue.

Nairobi has always served vegan and vegetarian cuisine, but exclusively vegan restaurants like Ethos in Westlands or Bridges in the Central Business District opened in 2023 to offer inviting animal-product-free menus.

If music be the food of love...

After the eerie silence of the pandemic years, Nairobi's live music scene has roared back to life. DJ nights are a dime a dozen, but if you really need to see someone pluck some strings or bang some drums, you will not be disappointed. Reggae, rap and rhumba are the most popular genres across the city, but note that Kenyan rhumba is actually a local flavour of the Congolese

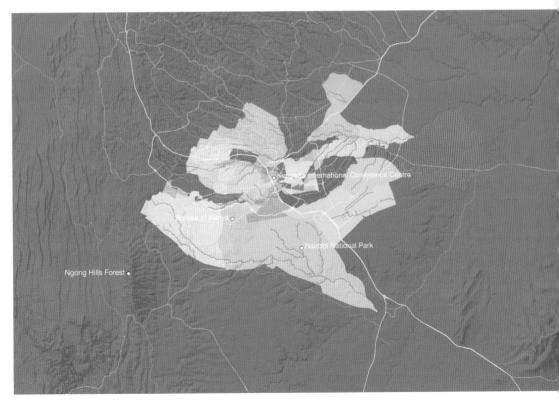

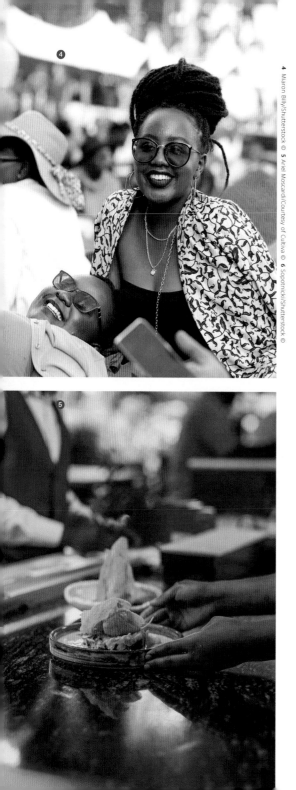

4 Miaron Billy/Shutterstock © 5 Ariel Moscardi/Courtesy of Cultiva © 6 Sopotnicki/Shutterstock ©

'Mutura', a type of African sausage, is peak Nairobi street food, especially after an epic night out. Get it from Tamu Tamu foods in Westlands, which also offers some of the best Swahili food in the city.

Blinky Bill, Nairobian musician

music that took the country by storm in the 1960s and has maintained a steady fanbase since. K1 in Westlands offers rhumba every Sunday afternoon, while in Lavington, Geco Café curates a steady rotation of talent across genres. After a short hiatus to regroup, the quarterly Blankets & Wine festivals at the Kasarani Stadium are building up to 2024 as their biggest year yet. And if you just want a taste of traditional music, the Bomas of Kenya in Karen features professional troupes offering daily performances.

A feast for the eyes

Art lovers rejoice! Local artists have been humming along for decades, with veterans developing distinct styles like the Tingatinga School. In recent years, a local collecting scene has emerged, with each year of the East African Art Auction being its best yet. Art spaces have taken notice, and even the Nairobi National Museum, once infamous for its musty collection of stuffed animals, today dedicates multiple rooms to contemporary shows and thought-provoking installations. Stay within the grounds for the small but mighty botanical garden

featuring an African medicinal plant garden, and a nature trail brimming with birdlife. At the Nairobi Gallery in the Central Business District, take a peek into the life of Joseph Murumbi, Kenya's second vice president and owner of the largest-known collection of African textiles, stamps and jewellery. Contemporary art rotates across the city including at the One Off Contemporary Art Gallery in Rosslyn, featuring a stunning sculpture garden, or the Circle Art Gallery in Lavington, while collective Brush Tu Gallery in BuruBuru also hosts visitors by appointment.

1 Nairobi National Park begins where the city ends 2 Fresh bread baked at Cultiva 3 Tropical fruits are easy to find 4 Enjoying the Blankets & Wine festival 5 Food fresh from the Cultiva kitchen 6 Uhuru Park and City Square at Nairobi's heart

Getting there

Nairobi is a pan-African hub for air travel, with further direct flights from European and Asian cities, plus New York.

When to go

There really isn't a bad time to be in Nairobi, but the best is between September and November, when jacaranda trees are in bloom and animals are migrating back into the adjoining national park.

Further reading

Yvonne Adhiambo Owuor's *Dust* has staggering lyricism, and Wanjiku Koinange's *The Havoc of Choice* offers grim witness to a difficult period. Makena Maganjo's *South B's Finest* is a hilarious local favourite.

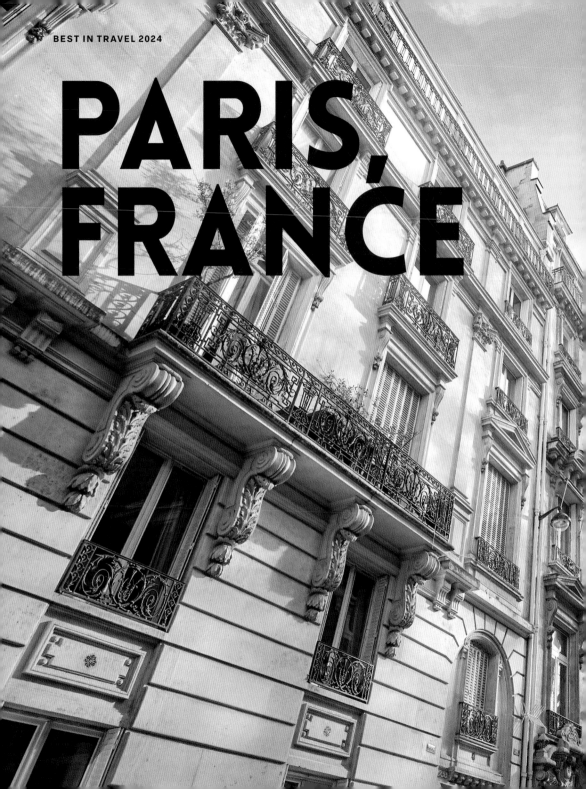

PARIS, FRANCE

As a spectacular world stage for the 2024 Summer Olympics and Paralympics, all eyes are on Paris. Cycling time trials will spin through town; beach volleyball and blind football will unfurl beneath the Eiffel Tower; and break-dancers will six-step to DJ beats across the square where Louis XVI's head rolled in 1793. Yet as a city constantly reinventing the wheel – a pharmacy prescribing books, photography exhibitions afloat the Seine, a triangle-shaped glass skyscraper – Paris raises the curtain on a buffet of innovations outside the sporting arena that also warrant your full attention.

1 James O'Neil/Shutterstock © 2 River Thompson/Lonely Planet ©

Highlights

01 **Be surprised by modern art** at Collection Pinault in the Bourse de Commerce, a former grain market and stock exchange.

02 **Hunt for flea-market treasures** and go for a feast in the new gourmet food court at the Marché aux Puces de St-Ouen.

03 **Admire 17th-century garden design** and Monet's waterlilies on murals in the elegant Jardin des Tuileries in the city centre.

04 **Clink rooftop cocktails** at Le Perchoir, with branches in the hipster 11e or on Europe's largest urban farm in the 15e.

3 iDrone Aerials/Shutterstock ©

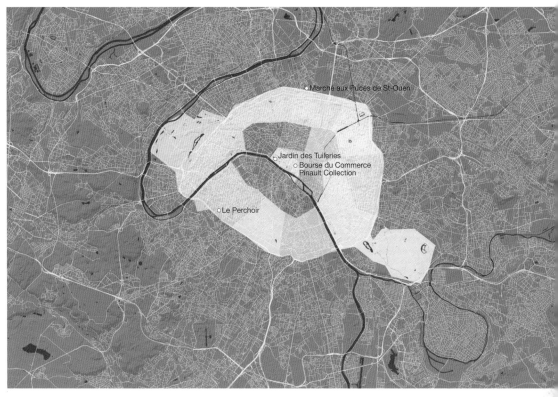

Marche aux Puces de St-Ouen

Jardin des Tuileries
Bourse du Commerce
Pinault Collection

Le Perchoir

Exploring alternative perspectives

The Olympics are a once-in-a-lifetime chance to experience icons known the world over – the Seine, Eiffel Tower – from a unique perspective. They also see the French capital write Olympic history again: it was in Paris in 1900 that women competed in the Games for the first time, and gender equality scores another coup this summer with equal numbers of male and female athletes taking part. Paris also aspires to inspire youth with four new Olympic disciplines: skateboarding, sport climbing, surfing and break-dancing. Neighbourhoods traditionally deemed insalubrious are enjoying new cachet as hosts to the Olympic Village (split between off-radar Saint-Denis, Saint-Ouen-sur-Seine and L'Île-Saint-Denis). What an opportunity to discover the real-life, non-touristy side of Paris.

New cultural pickings

Hot on the heels of several brilliant museum openings last year - Musée National de la Marine, Maison Gainsbourg, Quai de la Photo, Cité de l'Histoire at La Défense and, for mathematics geeks, La Maison Poincaré - all eyes are on Notre Dame. Shut since 2019 following a devastating fire, the emblematic cathedral with its sublime rose windows and bell towers reopens, if all goes to plan, in 2024. The architectural razzle-dazzle continues at top-drawer Olympic venue Grand Palais, with its Art Nouveau glass roof even more breathtaking after a €466 million renovation.

4 River Thompson/Lonely Planet © 5 River Thompson/Lonely Planet © 6 HUANG Zheng/Shutterstock ©

Hunting Invader's ceramic-tile mosaics with the FlashInvaders app takes players to side streets, busy and quiet neighbourhoods, even to the top of the Eiffel Tower. It makes me explore the entire city. I'm obsessed!

Elodie Berta, Parisian tour guide

For contemporary-art lovers, the new HQ of Fondation Cartier - handily close to the Louvre inside the historic Louvre des Antiquaires (1852) - is this year's little-black-book address.

Greener living

Paris mayor Anne Hidalgo continues to green the city, curb car traffic and tackle pollution. As of 2024, diesel cars are banned in the city, as is non-essential motorised through-traffic in the centre - pure joy for green-thinking visitors intent on mooching around museums and boutiques in neighbourhoods such as the Marais and the Latin Quarter. But then, this is the European city that almost single-handedly invented *flânerie* (seductive, indulgent promenading at leisure). In addition to 1000km (620 miles) of cycling lanes already servicing the capital, 60km (37 miles) of new dedicated bike lanes will link Olympic venues. By spring, metro line 11 should extend to Romainville, Montreuil, Noisy-le-Sec and Rosny-sous-Bois, easing commutes and opening up the northeastern edge of Greater Paris to curious visitors keen to uncover unexpected village-like quarters where few tourists tread.

Green spaces are popping up like mushrooms after the rain: on rooftops and walls, as urban forests, farms and moonlit gardens. In May, the first phase of a six-year makeover to transform the traffic-clogged Champs-Élysées into a green avenue kicks off with intensive tree planting and widening of pavements. And around the Eiffel Tower, parks, reflecting pools and an amphitheatre are being landscaped. Don't miss the reworked Pont d'Iéna bridge over the Seine – now a romantic greenway with sumptuous views.

1 The big reveal at the end of Rue de l'Université
2 Skateboarders on Place de la République 3 Twelve streets converge on the Arc de Triomphe 4 Boating on the Canal de l'Ourcq at Parc de la Villette 5 Village St Paul in the Marais neighbourhood 6 Jean Nouvel's Philharmonie de Paris in Parc de la Villette

Getting there

By plane to Charles de Gaulle or Orly (connected by bus, RER and/or metro to central Paris); Eurostar from London to Gare du Nord; or aboard a new Midnight Trains sleeper from Madrid, Milan or Berlin.

When to go

May, June, September and October promise pleasant temperatures, fewer queues and cultural events galore. For Olympic action: 26 Jul–11 Aug; the Paralympics 28 Aug–8 Sep.

Further reading

The New Parisienne by Lindsey Tramuta: the women and ideas shaping Paris. Sweet Paris by Frank Adrian Barron: recipes and style notes on Parisian patisserie and desserts.

MONTRÉAL, CANADA

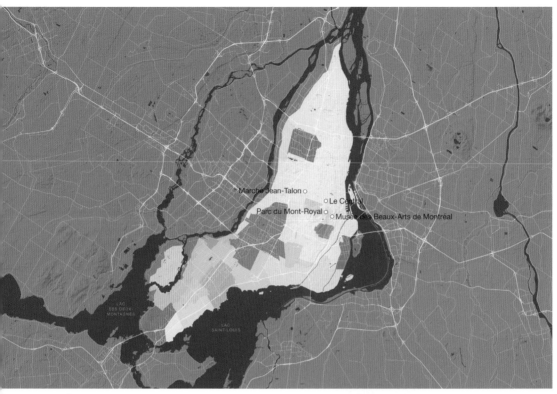

03

Marché Jean-Talon o
o Le Central
Parc du Mont-Royal o o Musée des Beaux-Arts de Montréal

LAC
DES DEUX-
MONTAGNES

LAC
SAINT-LOUIS

From an all-season calendar of festivals and arts events to revitalising neighbourhoods packed with diverse restaurants, *au courant* galleries and quirky shops, Montréal has long been one of Canada's coolest destinations. But this year, with new museums, revamped attractions, an ever-vibrant restaurant scene and added transport options making it even easier to reach, this metropolitan region of more than four million people, with its urban core set on an island where the St Lawrence and Ottawa rivers meet, is gearing up for far more fun.

New looks for local icons

Located on the traditional territory of the Kanien'kehá:ka peoples, Montréal today is home to a multicultural mix of populations that influence the arts scene of Canada's second-largest city, and Québec's biggest. The city's first Indigenous-artist-run centre, daphne, has reopened in a new gallery space showcasing works by the region's Indigenous artists. The 2024 edition of the Contemporary Native Art Biennial, known as BACA, will come to the city in May and June. To learn more about Québec's Indigenous communities, spend time in the carefully curated permanent exhibition, 'Indigenous Voices of Today: Knowledge, Trauma, Resilience', at the Musée McCord Stewart, devoted to Canadian history.

Le MEM, Centre des Mémoires Montréalaises, is the city's museum of stories. Formerly known as Centre d'histoire de Montréal, it's opening a new facility in the Quartier des Spectacles just north of downtown, where it will share multimedia histories of the region's residents.

Parc Jean-Drapeau welcomed the world more than 50 years ago for Expo 67, with its now-landmark geodesic dome designed by architect Richard Buckminster Fuller. Set on Île Sainte-Hélène in the St Lawrence River, the park is in the midst of a multi-year redevelopment slated to run until 2030, with ongoing improvements ranging from 15km (9 miles) of riverfront walkways to restored gardens and beaches.

Another urban icon scheduled to reopen in 2024 after a major renovation is the Montréal Tower, the tallest inclined tower in the world, where the vistas from its Olympic Park observatory extend across the city. Want

Highlights

01 **There's always something new** at Musée des Beaux-Arts de Montréal, whether you're into classical or contemporary art.

02 **For views across the city,** wander the green oasis of Parc du Mont-Royal on Montreal's 'mountain'.

03 **Go beyond poutine** at dining spots including French-Moroccan Nili, modern Korean 9 Tail Fox, and forager-favourite Anemone.

04 **Other culinary highlights** are the city's markets, from classics like Marché Jean-Talon to newer options like gourmet Le Central.

4

Getting there

Montréal-Trudeau (aka Dorval) is currently the city's only airport served by international flights, including many from Europe.

When to go

Montréal's busy events calendar keeps up through hottest and coldest months alike.

Further reading

Prep for your trip with titles including Mordecai Richler's *The Apprenticeship of Duddy Kravitz*, set in the city's 20th-century Jewish community; *Ru*, by Saigon-born, Québec-raised Kim Thúy; *The Fat Woman Next Door Is Pregnant* by Michel Tremblay, based in the Plateau neighbourhood; and *Lullabies for Little Criminals* by Heather O'Neill.

more sky-high views? Check out the recently completed, ultra-modern Tour du Port de Montréal at the waterfront Grand Quay.

Festivals year-round

Montréal loves a party. No matter what time of year you visit Canada's second-largest city, you're sure to find a festival, street fair or special event. Winter warms up with the annual Montréal en Lumière art and light fest; La Poutine Week, where you can sample numerous variations on Québec's fried potato, cheese and gravy-laden classic; and Igloofest, nicknamed 'the coldest music festival in the world'.

In the warmer months, you'll find festivals celebrating beer, public art, comedy, the region's Indigenous peoples, the LGBTQI+ community and more. With thousands of murals, the

Montréal is all about love, passion, and community. You can travel the world and sample the food of every continent via its vibrant cultural communities. Montréal took me in, fed me. Montréal made me who I am.

Chef Paul Toussaint, Kamúy Restaurant

street-art scene remains active, especially along Saint-Laurent Blvd, with additional outdoor art created every year during the summer MURAL fest. Launched more than 40 years ago and now the world's largest jazz fest, the Festival International de Jazz de Montréal continues to draw music-lovers every summer. And with Porter Airlines slated to open a Canadian hub at the city's smaller Saint-Hubert Airport east of the centre, and Amtrak resuming its US-Canadian Adirondack train, linking Montréal with New York City, getting to the festivals will become that bit easier for everyone.

1 Autumn in Parc du Mont-Royal **2** Poutine is most appreciated in Québec winters **3** A Tam-Tams drum circle at the George-Étienne Cartier Monument **4** Île Sainte-Hélène with the iconic Montréal Biosphere **5** The colourful Palais des Congrès **6** 'Gardens of Light' at the Montréal Botanical Garden

MOSTAR, BOSNIA AND HERCEGOVINA

1 Federica Gentile/Getty Images © 2 CHUNYIP WONG/Getty Images ©

Mostar is having a moment. A long-time favourite among backpackers and lovers of the Balkans, the city is finally registering as a destination that's worth more than a quick day trip. And while it may be the unforgettably scenic, minaret-dotted medieval Old Town and infamous bridge that draw visitors, it's the dynamic arts, crafts and music festivals that keep people longing to revisit. With the 20th anniversary of the reconstruction of the Stari Most bridge coming up this summer, there's never been a more jubilant time to go.

The creative quarter

After strolling the winding cobbled alleys past mosques, bazaars and cafes in the Old Town, be

Highlights

01 **The monumental Ottoman-era** buildings are some of Europe's finest examples of Islamic architecture. Koski Mehmed Paša Mosque, Kajtaz House, Sevri Hadži Hasan Mosque and Biscevic House are unmissable, as is the serene Dervish House is just 20 minutes out of town.

02 **Grab a slice** of *burek*. This moreish pastry, originally from Turkey, is a staple across former Ottoman Empire countries – and Bosnia's is known to be the best in the Balkans. The best in town can be found at Buregdžinica Rođeni. Choose between cheese, spinach or meaty fillings.

03 **A day trip** to the popular Kravica Waterfall is always a good idea, but if you're on a budget head instead to the smaller Koćuša Waterfall, which is free to visit.

3 Florin Cnejevic/Shutterstock ©

sure to cross the bright turquoise Neretva River to Španjolski Trg in the leafy western quarter of the city, where Street Arts Festival Mostar has been commissioning artists and designers to paint large-scale murals across the neighbourhood. With the intention of rebuilding community spirit and putting aside past conflicts, SAFMO invites local and international creatives to paint political, colourful, moving pieces. These large-scale works on abandoned buildings, residential blocks and urban spaces (which in some cases still have evidence of shelling from the heavy fire the city took during the Yugoslav Wars) have also helped to regenerate the area. While SAFMO unveils new work every summer, much of the art stays put year-round, so loop past Španjolski Trg no matter

when you visit. The square also hosts the Mostar Summer Fest, a three-day programme of bands from across the Balkans, and come December it's dotted with stalls selling food, arts and crafts at Mostar's Advent Christmas Market.

Sip back and relax
Delectable new wine tours of Mostar and the surrounding area are popping up following the European Union's sponsorship of the Wine Route of Hercegovina. Expert guides lead sensory adventures on one- or two-day tours, waltzing you round a handful of the 20-plus vineyards and wineries. Winemakers ferment their own grapes to produce one of two local wines: dense red Blatina or fresh white Žilavka. Aside from being

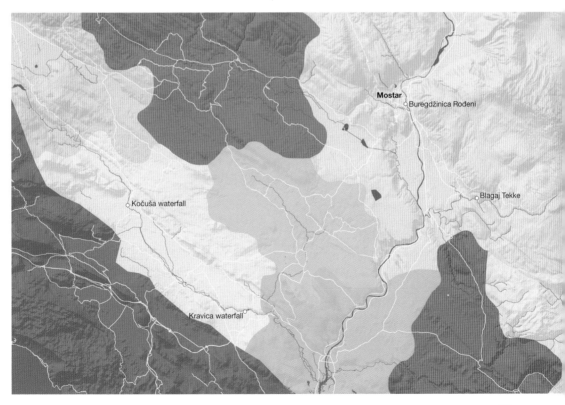

Mostar feels more Mediterranean than Sarajevo; Hercegovinian people are laid-back, warm and friendly. They're always happy to chat. People should use Mostar as their base to explore the region, it's got everything: boutique wineries, waterfalls and medieval villages like Počitelj and Blagaj.

Kathi Numić, co-founder of Cheyf Tours, Bosnia & Hercegovina

enjoyably cost-effective, these wine tours can also claim exclusivity, as both Blatina and Žilavka are not widely exported, so are hard to sample outside the country.

Bridging the gap

The city is quite literally named after its Stari Most (Old Bridge), so it's no surprise that people flock to see this emblem of Mostar. A source of pride since it was first constructed by the Ottoman Turks over 450 years ago, it's a moving sight, with one sweeping arch spanning the deep greens of the Neretva River. In 1993, the bridge was destroyed during the Yugoslav Wars. Restoration took three years and it was reopened to its former glory on 23 July 2004. Huge celebrations will be afoot this summer to mark its 20th anniversary, and its place as the

country's most iconic structure. For a thrilling spectacle, rock into town on the last weekend in July to watch the annual Mostar Bridge Jumping Festival – heir to a centuries-old local tradition. In recent years, Red Bull has also got involved and held a leg of its international cliff-jumping tournament here every August, with the public cheering on the world's bravest divers. To do the jump yourself (though we do not recommend it) you need to join the Mostar Bridge Jumping Club, who ask you to sign a few papers, pay an €25 fee, and off you go.

1 The Kravica Waterfall is a popular out-of-town sight
2 Lamps in a Mostar market 3 Koski Mehmed Paša
Mosque 4 Spiral-shaped *burek* is Bosnia's answer
to Turkish *börek* 5 A quieter day at Stari Most 6 The
bridge attracts divers, both pro and amateur

Getting there

Mostar has its own small airport, mostly for pilgrims headed to nearby Međugorje, but buses from Dubrovnik or Sarajevo provide more regular access.

When to go

Summer has a huge vibe, with festivals aplenty, but expect the city centre to be pretty busy, as many Bosnians have their second, seasonal home there – plus of course it's the most popular time of year to travel. If you prefer to visit when it's a little quiet, May–June or late September could be for you; if you like the idea of having the cobbled streets pretty much to yourself, the Christmas Advent Market in December is chilly but heartwarming.

PHILADELPHIA, USA

05

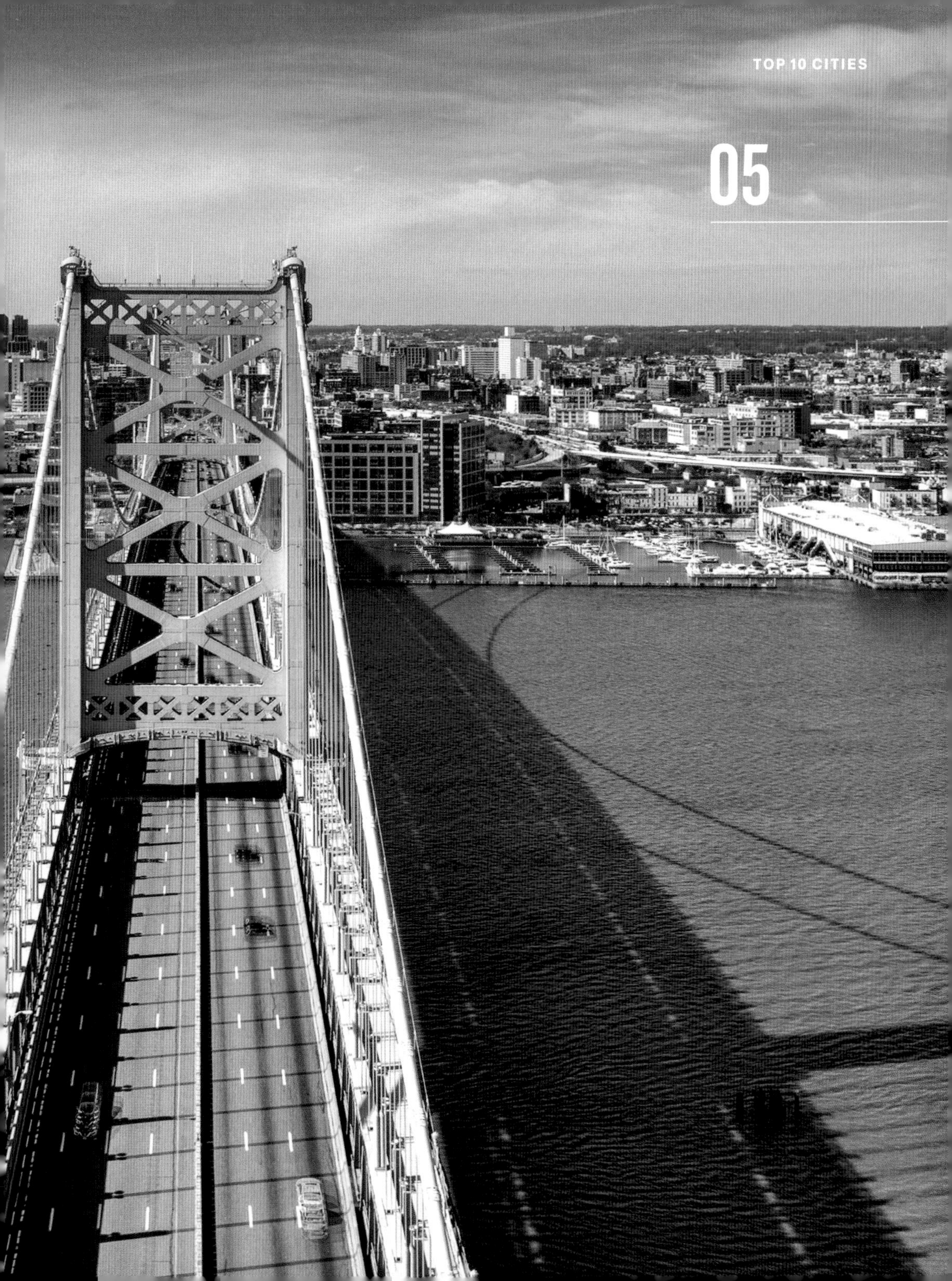

At the confluence of the Delaware and Schuylkill rivers sits the nation's first World Heritage City, aka the 'Cradle of Liberty', the birthplace of the United States and the 'City of Brotherly Love'. But what can get lost in all that historic high-mindedness is modern Philly's kinetic energy – and tectonically shifting cultural core. Between major new openings and milestone anniversary events, the museums alone warrant a trip in 2024. Then again, so do the eateries that will keep you fuelled for your museum marathon.

Halls of fame

Broad, leafy and lined with several hallowed institutions, the Benjamin Franklin Pkwy is the logical start to any local-culture binge.

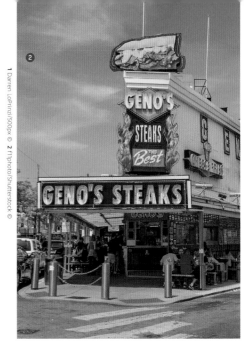

Highlights

01 **Roam the historic Italian Market** area for antipasti at Di Bruno Bros, tacos at South Philly Barbacoa, and a clash of cheesesteak titans.

02 **Newly legit** after years as an ad-hoc outfit, the Southeast Asian Market (Apr–Oct) has Cambodian, Lao, Thai and Vietnamese cuisine.

03 **In the Reading Terminal Market** halls, find Bassetts ice cream, Dutch Eating Place apple dumplings, and Termini Bros cannoli.

04 **Book at Zahav,** Michael Solomonov's empire-launching palace of mezze, *salatim* and *al ha'esh* delights.

Towards one end of this museum mile sits the Franklin Institute, a self-styled 'Wonderland of Science' that turns 200 in 2024, celebrating with made-over galleries, including the physiology exhibit that surrounds the literal beating heart of the institute. This beloved walk-through vital organ will remain intact, but everything around it will be swapped out for the most tech-forward and interactive displays. You'll also find overhauled Space galleries and a new Collections gallery, where you can explore Wright Brothers memorabilia, a 350-ton steam locomotive, and more or less every gizmo in between.

Steps away sits the Barnes Foundation, home to a collection like nothing you've ever seen - unless there's someone exceedingly flush, ambitious and quirky in your life who's amassed a staggering array of masterpieces and tchotchkes, and decided to display everything together in a series of patterned 'ensembles'. No? Then don't miss this bequest by the late Dr Albert C Barnes, a trove that includes - among other treasures - the world's largest Renoir and Cézanne collections. The 2024 bonus? A special exhibition about the celebrated photographer and art director Alexey Brodovitch.

Homegrown talent

At the same time, the Barnes will be operating the buzziest newcomer to the parkway in recent memory: Calder Gardens, projected for completion by late 2024. A joint undertaking of the Calder Foundation, philanthropists and government agencies, this ode to one of Philadelphia's

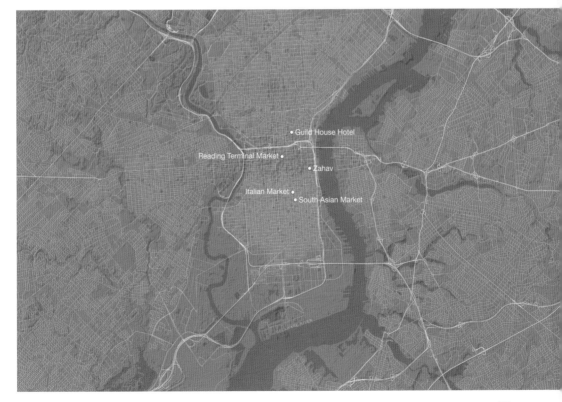

I love the Southeast Asian Market food in FDR Park, especially the stuffed wings. They look like normal wings but pack chicken meat, noodles and mushrooms marinated with Cambodian kroeung and herbs– a juicy flavour bomb.

Sarun S Chan, Cambodian Association of Greater Philadelphia executive director

favourite sons will set Alexander Calder's epic mobiles, 'stabiles', sculptures and paintings against the Pritzker Prize-winning architecture of Herzog & de Meuron – and the dreamy landscaping of Piet Oudolf (of NYC High Line fame).

Calder was the third generation of his family to create monumental works for the city – and nowhere is that lineage more dramatic than the parkway. Head to the window atop Great Stair Hall at the Philadelphia Museum of Art, where Calder's famed *Ghost* mobile hangs. Then look outside and you'll see his father's fountain in Logan Square and beyond that, the William Penn sculpture by grandpa Calder crowning City Hall.

In the spring of 2024, the Philadelphia Museum of Art will honour another local titan with 'Mary Cassatt at Work', the first large-scale American exhibition of her paintings in this century. Of course, the permanent collection includes countless other treasures, notably, the world's largest Duchamp collection.

Revolutionary ideas

Old City is no less happening in 2024, with an exhibition at the Museum of the American Revolution that tells the improbable backstory of George Washington's war tent. While you're there, admire the Forten family Bible, a highlight of the 2023 Black Founders exhibition. At the nearby Betsy Ross House, a succession of 250th anniversaries is bringing special events from late 2023 into late 2024. A particularly fun one: Tipsy History, a nighttime retelling of an 18th-century love story, with 250th anniversary cocktails.

1 Crossing the Delaware on the Benjamin Franklin Bridge **2** A cheesesteak classic on 9th St **3** The Philadelphia Museum of Art overlooks the Schuylkill River **4** Find a cross-section of global cuisines in town **5** The 21st-century home of the Barnes Foundation **6** Looking up Broad St to City Hall

Getting there

Philadelphia is served by flights from across North America and Europe, and Amtrak train services as far as Chicago and New Orleans.

When to go

Philly is hopping year-round – even in the dead of winter, when City Hall turns into a dazzling ice-skating-rink backdrop.

Further reading

For immersion into all things local, listen to DJ Jazzy Jeff, Boyz II Men, The Roots and Al Martino. Read Jennifer Weiner's *In Her Shoes* and Ann Patchett's *The Dutch House*. Watch *Silver Linings Playbook*, *Abbott Elementary*, *Concrete Cowboy*, *Rocky* – and if you're a fan of Old Hollywood, *The Philadelphia Story*.

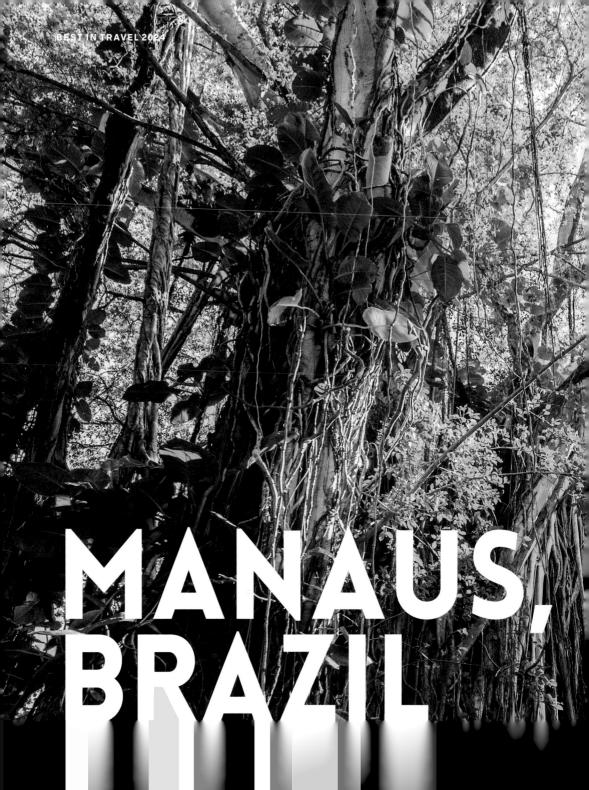

MANAUS, BRAZIL

Praia da Lua

RIO NEGRO

Teatro Amazonas

Encontro das Águas

RIO SOLIMÕES

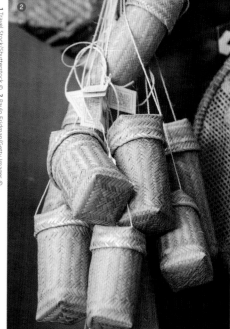

1 Travel Stock/Shutterstock © 2 Paulo Fridman/Getty Images ©

A poetic collision of steamy spectacle and ecotourism adventure awaits in Manaus. The Amazon region's largest city stands at the strangely unmixing confluence of the blackwater Rio Negro and the khaki-colored Rio Solimões, as the upper flow of the Amazon is called here. And surrounding it all is the world's largest rainforest, where countless unique and endangered species find their home.

Excitement is in the mist in Manaus, as the Amazon gears up to potentially play host to the United Nations Climate Change Conference in 2025. Along with its fellow Amazonian metropolis Belém, the most populous city in the jungle is a longstanding flashpoint in the ongoing struggle to save the rainforest. But while NGOs work tirelessly to clean up the city's *igarapés* (small streams and rivers) and ward off deforestation, the capital of Brazil's Amazonas state also finds itself exceptionally empowered to fight the good fight with sustainable tourism and Indigenous-led initiatives.

Sustainable river lodges

The further you travel from Manaus, the more upscale and isolated the options are (two of the best river lodges, Anavilhanas and Uakari, are several hundred kilometers away), but Manaus and surrounds do deliver chances to visit the rainforest sustainably much closer to the city. At Uiara Lodge, Indigenous guides lead guests on forest walkabouts and fascinating night tours around Lago Salvador, just 8km (5 miles) from Manaus, inspiring eco-tourists with stories of generations living off the land. Cabloco (mixed Indigenous/European ancestry) host Marilia Costa spent her childhood gallivanting around the 'Land of Guaraná', deep in the Amazon in Maués. Shaped by her upbringing as part Sateré-Mawé, her eight-room Manati Lodge focuses on rustic authenticity and strict, low-impact eco-tourism (no interactions with wild animals, no swimming with pink dolphins). Ecologically fished *tambaqui* and *tucunaré* highlight home-cooked meals prepared by a local chef. The sustainable architecture at top-end Juma Lodge reflects techniques employed in Indigenous homes. The lodge counts 90% of its staff from rainforest communities in its vicinity, is powered

Highlights

01 **Relive the rubber boom** at the Teatro Amazonas, Manaus' opera house and Belle Époque architectural superstar.

02 **Local ingredients** are paramount at Restaurante Banzeiro, an Amazonian dining destination from chef Felipe Schaedler.

03 **Only accessible by boat,** the floury, narrow river beach of Praia da Lua is the city's postcard-perfect patch of sand.

04 **Witness the magnificent meeting** of the waters, Encontro das Águas, where the powerhouse Negro and Solimões rivers clash.

by photovoltaic solar energy (panels that convert thermal energy into electricity) and employs its own biodigester, sewage treatment plant and recycling and waste centre. In the city itself, Adolpho Ducke Forest Reserve preserves the world's largest urban forest; and, across the Rio Negro, Parque Ecologico Janauari protects over 126 sq km (53 sq miles) of flooded forest, with giant water lilies and rare wildlife. Both are rainforest-light introductions to the surrounding 6.7 million sq km (2.6 million sq miles) of jungle.

Indigenous cuisine and restaurants

The Amazon's rich bounty delivers a cornucopia of flavours, textures and culinary experiences, nearly all of which are likely new to most palates. The Amazon palmberry, açai, is an antioxidant and iron-rich 'superfood' that has become trendy worldwide, but familiarity generally ends there. A stroll through the city's Mercado Municipal Adolpho Lisboa yields a cavalcade of novel tastes and aromas: fruity *tucumã* flakes, spicy *murupi* pepper, crunchy

Enjoy Manaus' rich fauna and flora on an open-air boat tour on the Rio Negro, stopping for lunch at a floating restaurant for quality regional food. Don't miss pirarucu or tambaqui on the barbeque!

Rodrigo Cunha, general manager, Hotel Juma Opera

ovinha flour (used to stuff fish or make *farofa* or couscous) and *tucupi*, a yellow juice extracted from wild manioc that's used in many regional dishes. The all-Indigenous menu at Brazil's first Indigenous-run restaurant, Biatüwi, showcases these gastronomic revelations of the Amazon basin (don't miss Sateré-Mawé chef Clarinda Ramos' spicy fish soup with black *tucupi* or *tambaqui* roasted in cocoa leaves). Look out for the city's signature sandwich: the *x-caboquinho* (curd cheese, fried *pacovã* banana and *tucumã* shavings on French bread). *Bom apetite!*

1 The richly biodiverse Amazon Rainforest surrounds Manaus **2** Local crafts at Anavilhanas **3** Teatro Amazonas dates from 1896 **4** Indigenous Amazonian cuisine **5** A wild toco toucan in the Brazilian Amazon **6** A riverboat crosses the Amazon River confluence

Getting there

Manaus Airport welcomes limited international flights – most travelers will connect in Rio de Janeiro or São Paulo. Long-distance riverboats run from numerous domestic destinations (Belém, Porto Velho, Santarém) as well as Leticia, Colombia.

When to go

The relatively dry months between June and mid-December are optimal for visiting the Amazon – especially for hiking. The annual Festival Amazonas de Ópera is held between March and May at the Teatro Amazonas.

Further reading

Márcio Souza and Milton Hatoum are the city's foremost authors on Amazon themes.

JAKARTA, INDONESIA

07

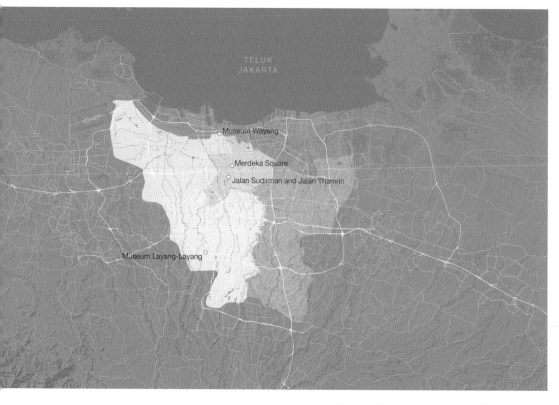

TELUK JAKARTA

Museum Wayang

Merdeka Square

Jalan Sudirman and Jalan Thamrin

Museum Layang-Layang

ndonesia's soon-to-be former capital has long been a base camp for international travellers going on to the nation's wild rainforests and far-flung islands. In 2022, the government announced that it would be moving to a newly built capital due to Jakarta's repeated flooding and infuriating traffic, but for many, this cosmopolitan city is still the place to indulge in urban comforts before venturing into the nation's remoter corners. While not known for its immaculate streets, its culture shines: decadent cocktails on sky-high rooftops, phenomenal global cuisine and forward-thinking galleries and museums. But things are likely to change with the new administrative centre – the planned capital of Nusantara will sit 1288km (800 miles) away on the island of

Borneo, likely taking many transport links, workers, and some of Jakarta's culture with it. 2024 is an opportunity to experience a historic and dynamic metropolis before the landscape changes forever. Here's where to start...

Eat your way around the world

Jakarta's dining scene punches well above its weight in terms of international flavours and sheer diversity of culinary offerings, for a fraction of the price of big cities like New York or Sydney. Here you'll find everything from glitzy shopping mall outlets like the Michelin-starred brand Din Tai Fung (offering perfectly paper-thin wrapped *xiao long bao* dumplings) to bowls of fresh Hawai'ian poke and tastebud-stretching local food. Night markets and food alleys are erected in the shadow of posh tower blocks to satisfy office workers. And for only a couple of dollars (try the outdoor food court Lenggang Jakarta) you can get a satisfying, filling and flavoursome plate of grub. Local food can be done fancy too, of course – eat *nasi goreng* (fried rice) and *roti bakar* (bread stuffed with cheese, sausage or eggs) at atmospheric traditional houses all over the city: try Plataran Menteng, an elegant old mansion with chandeliers and stately dining rooms.

Delve into coffee culture

Cafes to Jakartans are what pubs are to Brits, embedded in the culture and places to socialise with friends into the late hours. Caffeinated drinks are hugely sophisticated and respected

Highlights

01 **On Sunday mornings,** enjoy a stroll along stretches of Jalan Sudirman and Jalan Thamrin, empty of the usual swirl of cars.

02 **Zoom to the top** of the 132m-high (433ft) Monas tower in city-centre Merdeka Square, for soaring skyline views.

03 **Catch a weekend show** at Museum Wayang, with its intricate collection of some of the finest shadow puppets ever created.

04 **Hundreds of kite designs** hide in a mansion at Museum Layang-Layang – look for an enormous fish, and a horse and cart.

Getting there

Jakarta Soekarno-Hatta International is a hub for flights to Indonesia's multitude of islands (along with the smaller Halim Perdanakusuma Airport). It has international connections to Asian and Australian cities, plus Amsterdam and İstanbul.

When to go

Jakarta is best visited between June and September. Wet season, frequented by torrential rains, runs between October to April, peaking in January and February. Some 40% of the city sits below sea level, leaving it prone to serious flooding. It's also sinking an estimated 28cm (11in) a year in the northern areas; this, combined with rising sea levels, threatens future infrastructure problems.

in the city – most young locals know their Aeropresses from their nitro brews. There are micro roasteries all over the city, and with so many independent coffee shops, you needn't ever visit a chain. Artisan cafes come in all styles: colonial-esque with vintage furniture and jazz music playing (try Bakoel Koffie); uber-sleek and modern, where architects hang out (One Fifteenth Coffee); and the ones for true taste connoisseurs, serving single-origin beans from Indonesia (Tanamera Coffee).

Mall and market hop

Jakarta has more than 200 shopping malls – that's probably more than any other city on Earth – and it's here that all the city's resilient and friendly local populations collide. These labyrinthine air-conditioned spaces are packed with not only designer goods and high-street

I love the history of Jakarta. Everything started here and it's a melting pot of cultures and foods. The nightlife is also amazing – go club-hopping at Duck Down, Lucy in the Sky, Dragonfly, Billions and Embassy.

Ardy Wiraputra, Jakarta-born owner of The Packer Lodge

retailers but dozens of attractions: relaxing spas to hide from the whir of traffic outside, cinemas, karaoke booths, pulsating nightclubs and dancing fountains. There's even a giant Ferris wheel on the roof of the AEON Mall. It's hard to escape these giant retail villages during a trip to Jakarta, but don't forget to hit the streets themselves on two feet. Local markets (such as Chinatown's backstreet Petak Sembilan Market) and creative boutiques are dotted around the city (try dia.lo.gue artspace for independently designed arty products), while the vintage market (Pasar Antik) on Jalan Surabaya is crammed with wood carvings, retro items, antiques and jewellery.

1 Wisma 46 and other skyscrapers of central Jakarta
2 *Wayang kulit* is the best-known of Indonesia's forms of puppet theatre **3** Indonesian cuisine has a range of influences **4** The riverside Kampung Tongkol quarter **5** A footbridge across Jalan Sudirman by GBK City Park **6** Satay is a Javanese speciality

3 MARTIN WESTLAKE© 4 NurPhoto/Getty Images © 5 Wokephoto17/Shutterstock © 6 MARTIN WESTLAKE ©

PRAGUE, CZECH REPUBLIC

08

Prague is a pulsating European capital cloaked in a Gothic cityscape dating in parts from the 14th century. Iconic attractions like Prague Castle and Charles Bridge feel too beautiful to be real, and yet maybe too pretty for Prague's own good. In the past decade, visitors arrived in droves and partly spoiled the city's charms. The Covid-19 lockdown gave officials the chance to hit the reset button on runaway tourism. For 2024, they've promised a new emphasis on slow tourism, to rein in the numbers and promote attractions in residential areas away from the centre.

Exploring Prague's neighbourhoods

Most of Prague's world-class sights – Prague Castle, Charles Bridge, Old Town Square, the

1 Pyty/Shutterstock © 2 Francis Palma/Getty Images ©

Highlights

01 **Join locals** as they come to relax at Náplavka, a Saturday morning farmer's market on a pretty stretch of the Vltava riverbank.

02 **Art nouveau** Smetana Hall, inside Municipal House, is arguably Central Europe's most stunning concert venue.

03 **North of the centre**, Stromovka Park is an enormous expanse of manicured greenery, and a favourite spot for quiet walks.

04 **Enjoy a perfectly poured Pilsner** beer with accompaniments like goulash and bread dumplings at Lokál, a well-run pub.

3 Xantana/Getty Images ©

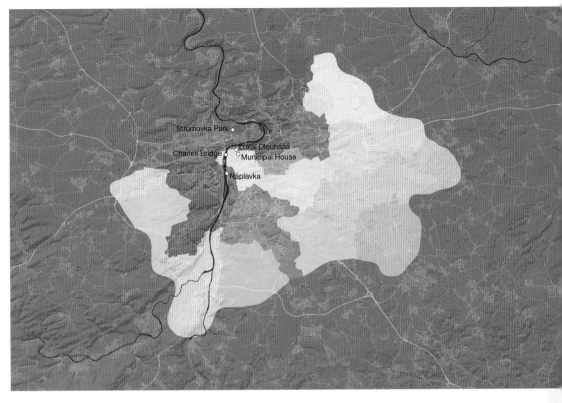

Astronomical Clock and Jewish Museum – occupy a compact area of the historic core. First-time visitors, understandably, will want to spend time here, walking the cobblestones and gawking at the medieval wonders that lurk around every corner. That said, Prague has much more to offer. A central element of the new slow tourism model is to encourage people to explore Prague's outlying areas – places where residents themselves go to enjoy their city.

Just south of the centre, the Vyšehrad Citadel occupies a serene pinnacle that attracts relatively few visitors. The fortress that stood here a millennium ago once rivalled Prague Castle in splendour. These days, the expansive parkland offers vistas out over the river and

an evocative cemetery, where the great 19th-century composers Antonín Dvořák and Bedřich Smetana, and art nouveau painter Alfons Mucha, among other notables, are buried.

Southeast of the centre, the leafy residential neighbourhood of Vinohrady, especially around metro stations Jiřího z Poděbrad and Náměstí Míru, features dozens of trendy cafes, wine bars, restaurants and pubs – and few tourists. Sample home-grown wines at the open-air Grebovka gazebo, in pretty Havlíčkovy Park.

North of the centre, across the Vltava River, the district of Holešovice is Prague's emerging art quarter. Anchored by the National Gallery's superb collection at the Trade Fair Palace and the newer DOX Centre for Contemporary

For authentic baked goods, try Perníčkův sen (Gingerbread Dream) in the Old Town to find traditional Bohemian gingerbread rolls, stuffed with plum jam and walnuts.

Eva Brejlová, tour guide for Eating Prague

Art, the area has seen an explosion in quirky galleries and one-of-a-kind boutiques, and is also home to Letná Park. These gardens occupy a steep bluff over the river, with postcard-worthy photo-ops and a beloved beer garden, where tourists and residents alike rub elbows in the open air.

Kafka remembered

The year 2024 marks the 100th anniversary of the passing of Prague-born author Franz Kafka (b 1883). Often hailed as the father of modern literature, Kafka died of tuberculosis at a sanatorium near Vienna on 3 June 1924. He was born in a house just off Old Town Square, and spent most of his life living and working at places around the Old Town. Kafka is buried at Prague's New Jewish Cemetery in the district of Žižkov, his tomb marked by a six-sided column, where a plaque also commemorates his three sisters, who died in the Holocaust.

Several institutions and museums, including the Prague Jewish Museum and DOX, are expected to hold exhibitions to commemorate the author's death. Another focal point will be the Franz Kafka Museum in Malá Strana.

Prague's relationship with its most-famous native son, over the years, has been complicated. Kafka was a Jewish author who wrote in German at a time when Prague was rapidly transitioning to a Czech-speaking city. Communist officials in the decades after WWII were highly uncomfortable with Kafka's themes of alienation and bureaucracy run amok. That said, local interest in Kafka's work has increased in recent years. For Kafka's part, Prague's presence is so palpable in his work it's almost as if the city forms a separate character.

1 The Vltava seen from Letná Park **2** Sedlec Ossuary in Kutná Hora outside town **3** Thirty statues line the parapets of Charles Bridge **4** A kinetic sculpture of Franz Kafka by the headline-grabbing artist David Černý **5** The Old Town Hall's Astronomical Clock **6** A hand-pulled ferry to an island in Stromovka Park

Getting there

Prague is easily accessible by rail or road from points all around Europe. Václav Havel Airport is the city's main hub for air travel.

When to go

Summer high season from June to August can get crowded and uncomfortably hot. Spring and autumn bring milder temperatures and often sunny weather, while winter sees a big drop in visitors and the chance to see Prague draped in snow.

Further reading

Primers include Franz Kafka's *The Castle*; *Prague Spring* by Simon Mawer; and *Under a Cruel Star* by Heda Margolius Kovály.

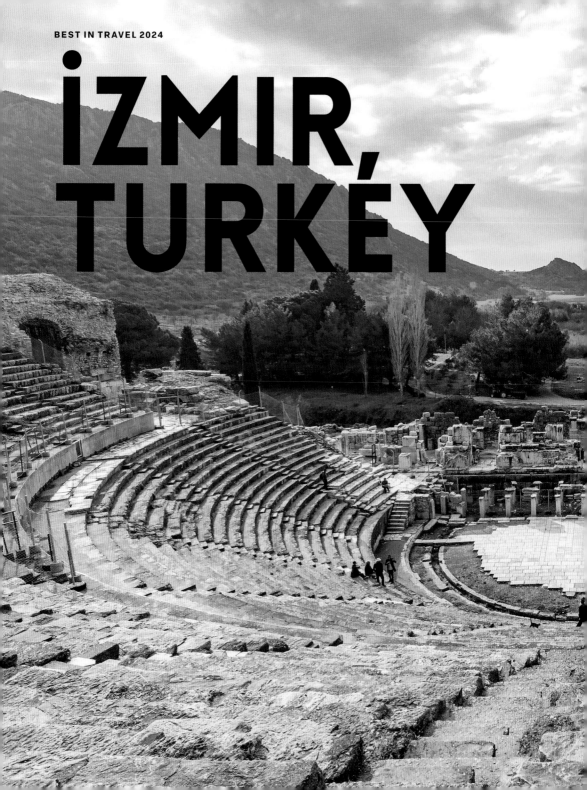

İZMIR, TURKEY

09

A city that prides itself on living the good life, İzmir often plays second fiddle to İstanbul, but with its seaside location, fresh Aegean cuisine, and blend of rediscovered heritage and revitalised contemporary culture, it merits its own turn in the spotlight. A lively old bazaar quarter, a popular annual music and dance festival, new arts and culture venues, a blossoming wine region, and easy access to beautiful beaches and ancient ruins are among the reasons to go before everyone else does.

Turkey's third-largest city, seaside İzmir has a relaxed, convivial vibe that's been luring residents away from hectic İstanbul in recent years. Its charms, though, are still waiting to be

1 Nejdet Duzen/Shutterstock © 2 ernhkm/Getty Images ©

3 Hatice Bakcepinar/Shutterstock ©

Highlights

01 Have a seaside meal of fresh fish and *meze* (small plates) with free-flowing *rakı* (anise spirit) at Balıkçı Hasan, Deniz or Veli Usta.

02 There's always more to discover while winding through the historical Kemeraltı bazaar district, with shops of every variety.

03 The İzmir Festival brings concerts and dance performances each June/July to unique venues such as the ancient Roman agora.

04 Taste local wines from small boutique vintners amid the rolling hills of Urla, west along the coast.

discovered by most international visitors, who know the city - if at all - as a brief port of call on a cruise or as a gateway to the rightfully famous ancient Greek and Roman ruins at Ephesus.

İzmir's beating heart is its Kordonboyu, a 1.7km-long (1 mile) esplanade along a broad bay where locals promenade and play in the city's reputed 300-per-year days of sunshine. Eating (and drinking) well is a way of life here, and İzmirites have a particular passion for dishes cooked with the region's olive oil, including a wide variety of wild Aegean herbs and other greens (collectively known as *ot*). The cuisine melds influences from the Greek, Levantine and Jewish communities that predominated in the

city (previously known as Smyrna) before it was devastated by war and a massive fire in 1922.

From ancient to contemporary
Much of the city had to be rebuilt after the blaze, resulting in its modern appearance today, but İzmir has lately been rediscovering its history.

1 The Ancient Greek Great Theatre of Ephesus
2 Turkey is one of the world's largest producers of wine grapes **3** A bakery on Anafartalar Caddesi
4 The Roman agora of Smyrna, modern İzmir **5** The Vienna Chamber Orchestra performing at Ephesus
6 Coves along the Karaburun Peninsula coast

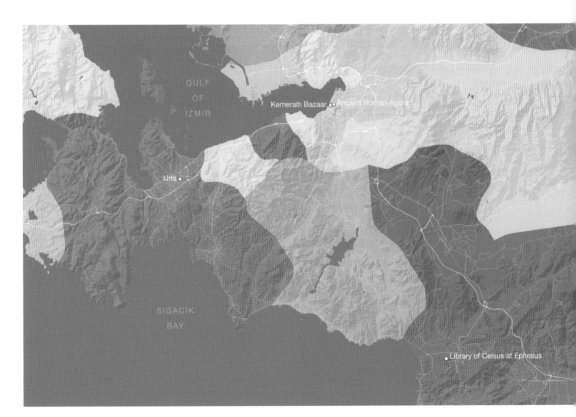

This is a hedonistic city; nothing happens before 10am and we're always out in the streets, eating, drinking and walking. The sky is usually blue and it just makes you feel good.

Nüket Franco, Culinary Backstreets tour guide

Some of the nine synagogues that once served congregations in the central Kemeraltı bazaar district are being restored, and new excavations are underway at the nearby Roman agora and at Kadifekale, a hilltop castle that dates to the 3rd century BCE. A recently uncovered ancient theatre between the agora and the castle is expected to open at least partially to visitors in 2024.

İzmir's contemporary culture is also gaining new vibrancy, with young artists setting up studios and independent art spaces like Darağaç and Çatı Açık Sanat Alanı in the formerly industrial Umurbey neighbourhood behind the Alsancak train station. They join more established cultural players like K2 Contemporary Art Center in the trendy Alsancak neighbourhood, and the Arkas Art Center in a century-old mansion along the waterfront. One former factory in Alsancak has already been converted into a culture and arts centre, and another is on the way; an inaugural İzmir Mediterranean Biennial is in the works too.

Roman ruins, fine wines and secluded beaches
As much as there is to do in the city these days, İzmir's location also makes it an excellent base for

exploring what the larger region has to offer. The stunning ruins of Ephesus, along with the pretty hilltop village of Şirince, the historic attractions of Selçuk and the Yedi Bilgeler vineyards, are only an hour's drive south. To the north lies the İzmir Bird Paradise, a wetland nature reserve home to more than 200 bird species including flamingos, storks and pelicans, as well as the bucolic seaside town of Foça.

West of İzmir, the Urla, Çeşme and Karaburun peninsulas jut out into the Aegean Sea, almost reaching the Greek island of Chios. Their sinuous coastlines are dappled with small beaches and resort towns. The windsurfing destination of Alaçatı is packed with chic boutique hotels and high-end dining, while Çeşme has a more unassuming, family-friendly vibe, and Urla can claim both a winery route and a burgeoning arts and crafts scene.

Getting there
Direct flights connect to İstanbul as well as European hubs like London and Frankfurt. It's a five-hour drive from İstanbul, or a leisurely train ride, transferring either in Eskişehir (14hr total trip) or in Balıkesir (via ferry to Bandırma, limited winter service, 9hr total).

When to go
İzmir is a year-round destination, with relatively mild winters and breezes off the bay alleviating the worst of summer heat.

Further reading
Paradise Lost: Smyrna, 1922 by journalist Giles Milton delves into tragic but crucial historic events; *The Ghosts of Smyrna* by Loren Edizel is a fictional saga exploring the same era.

KANSAS CITY, USA

10

Don't you dare dismiss this as flyover country. Thanks to the opening of a brand spanking new state-of-the-art airport terminal and the extension of the free-to-ride streetcar line through Kansas City's urban core, the 'Heart of America' is more firmly on travellers' maps than ever before. Logistics aside, KC has so much to shout about in 2024, from huge sporting firsts to grassroots efforts to revitalise its cityscape. Not that you'll hear residents gloating too much about the transformation taking place here – the commandments of 'Midwestern Nice' dictate humbleness after all.

You've certainly seen Kansas City on TV lately. Was it when the Kansas City Chiefs won two of

1 TriggerPhoto/Getty Images © 2 Raymond Boyd/Getty Images ©

3 Carmen Mandato/Getty Images ©

Highlights

01 **Go big on barbecue** – Ted Lasso's 'Joe Arthur Gatestack' T-shirt is an in-joke at the crux of KC's gluttonous dilemma, so try them all: Joe's, Arthur Bryant's, Gates and Jack Stack.

02 **Beyond burnt ends** – KC's food scene is increasingly diverse, and nationally recognised. Try authentic Palestinian food at Baba's Pantry and Mexican drinks at Café Ollama.

03 **During Prohibition**, Kansas City was called 'Paris of the Plains' because the flow of alcohol never ceased, thanks to political boss Tom Pendergast. The spirit (and spirits) of the era have been revived at distilleries such as J Rieger and Tom's Town.

the last four Super Bowls? Maybe it was tearing up during the Fab Five reveals on the two seasons of *Queer Eye* filmed in KC? Or perhaps you felt it in the irresistible charm of Jason Sudeikis, who grew up in Kansas City, cracking the stiff upper lips of those stoic Brits on *Ted Lasso*? The sightings won't stop there, but it's high time to come see KC for yourself.

Play on

The love of sports runs deep in the Midwest, and Kansas City is carving out its own niche as the 'Soccer Capital of America'. While the title might be self-proclaimed, it's not without merit: KC won a bid to host some of the World Cup 2026 games, the smallest of the 11 selected US metro areas.

And Kansas City is constructing the first purpose-built stadium for a National Women's Soccer League team, set to open for the 2024 season.

The new front door of Kansas City

February heralded the completion of the largest single infrastructure project in the city's history: the new terminal at Kansas City International Airport. KCI's thoughtful design features change

1 The revived KC Streetcar on Main St **2** 18th and Vine is the historic home of jazz in Kansas City **3** Skyy Moore of the Chiefs celebrates winning the 2023 Super Bowl **4** Kansas City serves one of the 'Big Four' US barbecue styles **5** Downtown KC **6** Echoes of Spain around Country Club Plaza

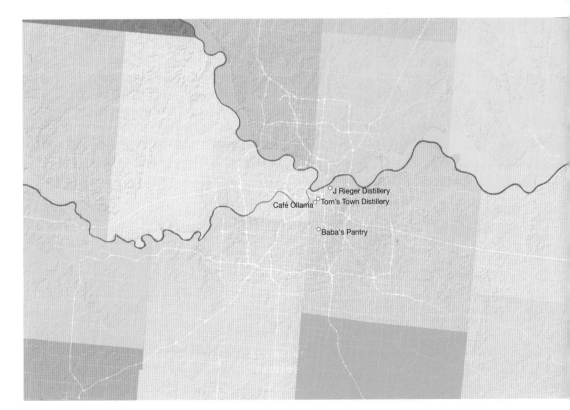

○ J Rieger Distillery
Café Ollama ○ ○ Tom's Town Distillery

○ Baba's Pantry

I love living in Kansas City because it has a rich history, a vibrant arts scene, and a supportive community that inspires my creativity and entrepreneurship.

Kemet Coleman, musician and co-founder of Vine Street Brewing Co.

the game on air travel. Red and green lights above toilet stalls and in the parking garage show what's available at a glance, and seating areas include wireless charging. Non-gender bathrooms, inclusive play areas and glass-walled jet bridges ensure that all feel welcome. Travellers with disabilities or those with autism, or those hesitant to fly, can book the Air Travel Experience simulator, the first of its kind at a US airport, that replicates the process of checking bags, going through security and boarding a flight without leaving the ground.

Airports are often a traveller's first experience of a place, and Kansas City's front door shows off its love of all things local. Ceilings are made of Missouri hemlock wood, and fossils are embedded in the walls of locally quarried limestone. More than $5.5 million was spent on art, and 19 of the 28 pieces were created by local artists. Along with some nationally known airport staples, 80% of vendors are local restaurants and breweries.

Rethinking KC's urban fabric

Car-centric sprawl has infected many midsize US cities, but KC has started to claw its way back. An extension to the KC Streetcar, which opened as a two-mile tram line through downtown, will be unveiled at the end of 2024, passing the Westport bar district, the world-class Nelson-

Atkins Museum of Art and the Country Club Plaza, a 100-year-old outdoor shopping area with Spanish architecture designed to look like Seville.

The historic Black neighbourhood of 18th and Vine, birthplace of Kansas City-style jazz, is breathing new life into abandoned structures, including an 1870s Water Department building that will house an art museum and Missouri's first Black-owned brewery.

Just as it straddles the state line, Kansas City sits at the confluence of the Kansas and Missouri rivers, and these once-ignored waterways are finally getting attention. The Rock Island Railway Bridge, opened in 1905, is being converted into an over-water entertainment district of restaurants and bars slated to open in 2024. High-flying plans for an aerial park and zipline course over the river, the first in the US to cross a state border, are also in the works.

Getting there

While the new airport terminal makes an impressive gateway (mostly domestic, with a few routes to Canada, Mexico and the Caribbean), Union Station in the heart of Kansas City is one of the most beautiful in the US. Opened in 1914 as the country's third-largest train station, it was built in beaux arts style. It has Amtrak services to St Louis, Chicago and Los Angeles. Nearly abandoned in the 1980s, the station marks its 25th anniversary of reopening in 2024.

When to go

Kansas City's middle-of-the-continent climate means hot, humid summers and January mostly below freezing. The NFL season runs September to January.

BEST IN TRAVEL 2024
TOP 10 REGIONS

Western Balkans' Trans Dinarica Cycling Route
Kangaroo Island, South Australia / Tuscany, Italy / Donegal, Ireland
País Vasco, Spain / Southern Thailand / Swahili Coast, Tanzania
Montana, USA / Saalfelden Leogang, Austria

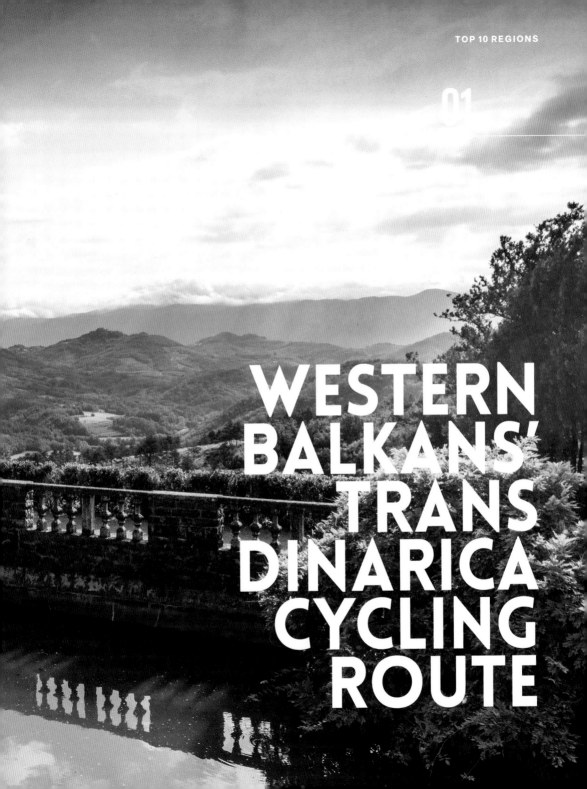

01

WESTERN BALKANS' TRANS DINARICA CYCLING ROUTE

The Trans Dinarica is the first bicycle route to connect the entire Western Balkans. However, the 80-stage itinerary, set to launch in 2024, is more than just a cycle-centric way to experience southeastern Europe's epic geography. Yes, the 3364km (2090-mile) trail – linking Slovenia, Croatia, Bosnia and Hercegovina, Montenegro, Albania, North Macedonia, Kosovo and Serbia – spotlights mountain ranges, the Adriatic Sea and a gluttony of lakes and rivers. But this moderate-difficulty, eight-country route (daily stages average 50km/31 miles) also prioritises the sustainable discovery of Unesco sites, national parks and villages loaded with ancient culture.

1 Uroš Švigelj / Courtesy GoodPlace © 2 Creative Travel Projects ©

3 Nataliia Budianska/Shutterstock ©

Highlights

01 **Before starting in Slovenia,** understand the region's history at the Kobarid Museum, dedicated to WWI's Isonzo (Soča) Front.

02 **The calling-card attraction** in Split, Croatia, is Diocletian's Palace – a Roman emperor's retirement villa dating back to 305 CE.

03 **Watch divers leap** from atop the famous Ottoman-era Mostar Bridge in Bosnia and Hercegovina, resurrected in 2004.

04 **Straddling the borders** of Albania and North Macedonia, Lake Ohrid is both a natural and cultural World Heritage Site.

Peaks and sea

The Trans Dinarica wastes no time pulling out a showstopping photo-op. The route starts in Kobarid, Slovenia (which Hemingway described in *A Farewell to Arms* as 'a clean little town' with 'a fine fountain in the square'), tucked in the Julian Alps on the southwestern edge of Triglav National Park and straddling the mesmerizingly celeste-green Soča River. The trail then heads south past the Unesco-inscribed Škocjan Caves before rolling into Croatia and the Adriatic city of Rijeka.

With the Dinaric Alps towering to your east and the Adriatic's cobalt blue to the west, the coast guides you on a combination of quiet asphalt roads and easy-going forest paths – typical of riding surfaces across the route. You'll pass through a corridor of six Croatian national parks, including waterfall-combed Plitvice Lakes and the rock-climbing haven of Paklenica. Along the way, the Roman-era, World Heritage cities of Zadar and Split remind you this is as much a cultural expedition as it is an active one.

Heart of adventure

For many cyclists, Bosnia and Hercegovina marks a step into the unknown – that delicious place where the unexpected fuels wide-eyed discovery. Entering this heart-shaped country also means pedalling into the heart of the Dinaric Alps, where ancient culture awaits. Both that pioneering spirit and the Trans Dinarica undulate through remote, welcoming villages before funnelling into the

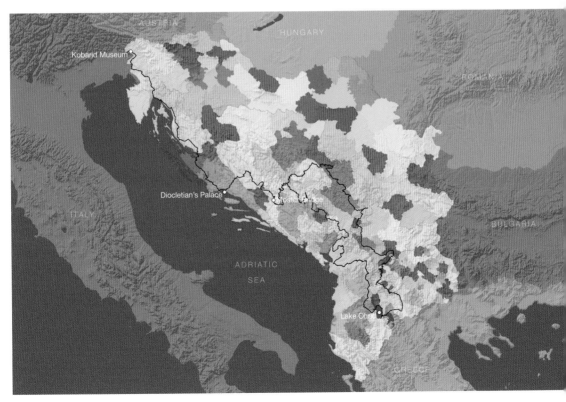

Cycling is the right way to see the Western Balkans. This region is perfect for travellers who combine adventure, culture and a glass of wine at the end of the day.

Jan Klavora, a Trans Dinarica Cycle Route designer

Neretva River valley down to the city of Mostar (see p96 for more), where daredevils dive from atop its Unesco-listed, Ottoman-era bridge.

Traditional fare such as *burek* (meat-filled pastry) and *ćevapi* (sausages served with pita) sustains riders into Montenegro along the Tara River Canyon, Europe's deepest gorge. Afterwards, they'll climb and descend to the country's own Unesco locale: Durmitor National Park, where the 2523m (8278ft) peak of Bobotov Kuk beckons. From here, cyclists make their way to the protected birdwatching paradise of Skadar Lake before entering Albania's Theth National Park and the grandeur of the 'Albanian Alps'. This splendour continues as the trail points south to Lake Ohrid, Europe's oldest lake, which has the rare distinction of being both a natural *and* cultural World Heritage Site.

Where empires meet

Pedalling into North Macedonia, from Lake Ohrid to Lake Prespa, on the Greek border, cyclists feel the weight of Balkan history. Travelling north, the route journeys through territory traded between kingdoms and empires for millennia. Ancient Greeks, Macedonians, Romans, Byzantines and Ottomans all contributed to a complex heritage.

After crossing into Kosovo, the path enters Prizren, where Ottoman architecture dominates this city bisected by the Lumbardh River in the foothills of the Sharr Mountains. Continuing north, the trail reaches Serbia, its eighth country. The route hugs Serbia's western border up to the ski-resort towns of Zlatibor and Mokra Gora. At Tara National Park, dense forests and the Drina River Canyon pilot cyclists. The Trans Dinarica then turns west into Bosnia to complete a loop of the lower six countries. In the historic capital Sarajevo, the call to prayer from minarets melds with church bells wafting above the Miljacka River to welcome back triumphant adventurers.

1 Rest stop in Slovenia 2 View from Đurđevića Tara Bridge, Montenegro 3 Split has grown from a Roman core 4 Riding Slovenia's Julian Alps 5 Braving the jump in Mostar 6 Tara River in Durmitor National Park

Getting there

The route provides access to all the Western Balkans' capitals. The most logical starting point is Ljubljana, Slovenia, where a 2.5hr train journey ushers cyclists to within a few miles of Trans Dinarica's trailhead.

When to go

Though the Trans Dinarica is doable for three-quarters of the year – besides winter – the best times are May to June and September to mid-October, when the weather is cool and stable.

What to ride

The route — a mix of quiet roads, packed gravel, and forest paths – was designed for all skill levels. Gravel bicycles work best here.

KANGAROO ISLAND, AUSTRÁLIA

02

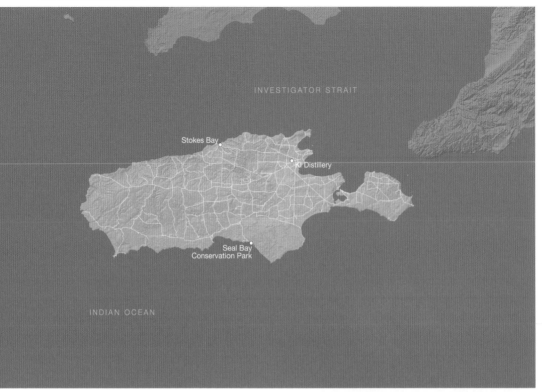

INVESTIGATOR STRAIT

Stokes Bay

KI Distillery

Seal Bay
Conservation Park

INDIAN OCEAN

There's an otherworldliness to Kangaroo Island – or KI as you'll hear locals refer to it – which dazzles, bewilders and intoxicates. A mere 40-minute flight from the South Australian capital Adelaide, KI is Australia's third-largest island, dwarfing the likes of Singapore or Bali, but is surprisingly isolated. Deceptively vast and blessed with a ridiculous amount of stunning coastline, 540km (335 miles) to be exact, this is where you may find you've scored the entire beach to yourself. Kangaroo Island invites guests to indulge in its unique local produce, encounter adorable Australian wildlife and discover some of the country's best beaches.

1 Meaghan Coles © 2 Phuong D. Nguyen/Shutterstock ©

The island sanctuary

A haven for wildlife, the island's isolation from the Australian mainland has helped it to become an ark for native and endangered species. You'll spot kangaroos jumping down the road, spy a koala casually nestling in the eucalypt canopy, or happen across the prickly yet adorable echidna as it quietly sashays through the scrub. The turquoise waters that surround Kangaroo Island are inhabited by dolphins, penguins and the rare leafy seadragon, and they offer awesome scuba and snorkelling experiences. The island is also home to one of Australia's largest sea lion colonies, and at the Seal Bay Conservation Park, visitors are permitted on a hosted beach walk where they can responsibly view these wild animals at rest and play.

Massive chunks of the island are crisscrossed by unsealed roads with little to no phone reception, ultimately revealing part of this place's magic: time here side-steps the chaos of the everyday and allows connection to the environment, devoid of distraction.

Remarkable renewal

The devastating Black Summer bushfires across 2019-2020 were the worst in the island's recorded history, scorching over half of the land. The toll on native animals, livestock and livelihoods was horrific and can't be understated. But the bush, like the islanders themselves, is a remarkable regenerator and recovery is evident everywhere. This provides visitors the unique opportunity to witness first-hand the

Highlights

01 **Take a gin-blending masterclass** at Australia's oldest dedicated gin distillery, KI Spirits, and walk away with a spicy or sweet little creation of your own.

02 **Clamber through** a narrow cave system at Stokes Bay that acts as the audacious entrance to one of Australia's best 'secret' beaches.

03 **Join a guided beach tour** at the Seal Bay Conservation Park, one of the world's largest – and smelliest – breeding colonies of endangered Australian sea lions. If you're lucky, you'll spy small pups that will melt the hardest of hearts.

Getting there

The car and passenger ferry to Kangaroo Island departs from Cape Jervis, and flying from Adelaide to Kingscote only takes 40 min with the route serviced daily.

When to go

The island is a total show-off during the Aussie summer (Jan–Feb) but also rewards those who venture there in early autumn (Mar–Apr) or spring (Sep–Nov).

Further reading

Molly Murn's *Heart of the Grass Tree* combines historical detail of the sealers who settled here in the 1800s with an uplifting tale of mothers and daughters acclimatising to a hypnotic yet harsh environment.

extraordinary revival of the landscape. On a drive through the vast Flinders Chase National Park, en route to see the island's big natural attractions, Remarkable Rocks and Admirals Arch, you'll witness massive bunches of vivid green foliage bursting from the base of blackened trees, whose twisted, naked branches seek out the sky. With a multi-million-dollar visitor centre set to reopen at the park's main entry point in 2024, the gateway to this regenerating garden will get a glittering new doorway.

Drinking in the scenery

It's clear that the island's recovery is an economic one as much as it is a natural one. In 2024, an increased passenger and vehicle ferry service from the mainland town of Cape Jervis to the cute coastal enclave of Penneshaw will allow

There is always something special to experience on the island, whether it's through stories from a farmer, producer or locals. To put all that onto a plate and share those stories through food and wine is even better.

Dylan & Yolandi Pitallo, owners and chefs at The Odd Plate

more travellers the opportunity to sample the island's epicurean delights.

Dining on KI is all about location, location, location. Whether it's settling in to sample a sparkling rosé at Bay of Shoals Winery while watching sailboats gently bob in the sheltered waters below the vines; discovering mouthwatering ice-cream, tangy beer or silky popcorn made with Australian bush honey from the world's purest strain of Ligurian bees; or indulging in Australia's most wild dining experience at 'Gastronomo', where grand gourmet meals are served under the enormous snaking limbs of a 120-year-old fig tree, Kangaroo Island is a place of magical wonder that seduces the senses while satisfying the belly.

1 Grape vines and safe anchorage at Bay of Shoals Winery **2** Looking under Admirals Arch in Flinders Chase National Park **3** Coastal views at Remarkable Rocks **4** Western River Cove on KI's north shore **5** A couple of Remarkable Rocks **6** Australian sea lion pups at Seal Bay Conservation Park

TUSCANY, ITALY

03

Few places celebrate the slow life or embody *la dolce vita* like Tuscany. Be it exploring new hiking trails or rediscovering *cucina contadina* (farmhouse cuisine), the new-gen Tuscan experience remains in perfect symbiosis with the land. Meanwhile, there are about 50 villages all around Tuscany where Etruscan heritage can be spotted, and in the rural valley of Valdichiana, archeologists are digging up the past to turn mindfulness mantras forged by the ancients into modern notions of self-care.

Rebirth in Etruscan-Roman history

Of equal excitement to the 24 Etruscan bronze statues unearthed in the medieval spa village of San Casciano dei Bagni in 2022 is the giddy

1 Stevanzz/Shutterstock © 2 Suttipong Sutiratanachai/Getty Images ©

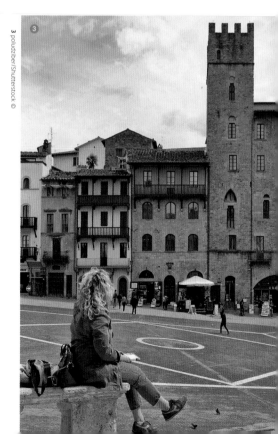

3 poludziber/Shutterstock ©

Highlights

01 **Marvel at unrivalled art**, from medieval to Renaissance, in the Duomo and Museo Civico in the hilltop city of Siena.

02 **Uncover the insatiable charm** of Arezzo over a *passeggiata* (afternoon stroll) and *aperitivo* (drinks) on cinematic Piazza Grande.

03 **Drink in** unmatched Valdichiana views at sunset over a glass of Vino Nobile at 19th-century Caffè Poliziano in Montepulciano.

04 **Watch the Tour de France,** the world's most famous cycling race, depart from Florence on 29 June 2024.

anticipation of what other priceless artefacts remain embalmed in the Tuscan mud. The dig at the village's antique thermal baths continues with newfound zeal as archeologists fastidiously inch their way across Il Santuario Ritrovato ('the Rediscovered Sanctuary'), which they only realised to be of monumental proportions last year.

Etruscans took to the waters here in the 2nd and 1st centuries BCE, bathing in pools fed by 42 natural hot springs and venerating deities who assured the thermal water's divine healing powers. Wealthy families commissioned local artisans to sculpt intricate statues of Apollo, Hygeia, Fortuna et al in bronze, dedicated to the sacred pools they safeguarded. Under bon vivant Romans from the 3rd century CE, the baths were enlarged and

became so notable that customised bronze, silver and orichalcum coins were minted specifically for Roman Emperor Augustus (c 62 BCE–14 CE) to offer to the gods in exchange for his good health. Pencil-sized votive bronzes of a swaddled baby, ears, limbs, a penis even, found in the 2022 stash reveal body parts and ailments that wellbeing-conscious Etruscans and Romans sought to pamper, soothe or heal in the curative waters. In 2024, guided tours led by local archeologists will herald a fully fledged archeological park.

Searching for resurrected souls
Admiring the Etruscan booty uncovered so far in San Casciano dei Bagni's new museum, to open in 2024 in 16th-century Palazzo dell'Arcipretura,

> *The time has finally come to make known so many hidden treasures, together with the myriad of wonders of the Tuscan land. The Uffizi Diffusi project brings artworks from our deposits back to the places where they were born.*

Eike Schmidt, museum director, Galleria degli Uffizi

will be an evocative waltz through a civilisation that remains enigmatic. A much-welcome sequel to Chiusi's Museo Civico 'La Città Sotterranea' (which explores Etruscan inscriptions) and the riveting displays on Etruscan women in Chianciano Terme's Museo Archeologico, the new museum might shed light on why exactly these well-dressed Etruscans with elaborate hairdos headed to Tuscany in the 9th century BCE.

One glance at the golden wheat fields and flower-spun pastures, forests thick with wild boar and sun-drenched vineyards ribboning Valdichiana's softly rolling hills makes it easy to understand why they stayed. San Casciano's hilltop flourish of medieval stone houses crowned by the bell tower of Chiesa di San Leonardo screams Tuscany, as does the valley's timeless scattering of km-zero farmer's markets and *trattorie*, fueled more ruthlessly than ever with local produce: top-drawer Chianina beef from the valley's native cows, tomato-crusted *pecorino rosso* cheese and red Vino Nobile di

Montepulciano wines, best tasted at source along a vineyard-stitched walking, e-biking or horseback trail. By 2024 several dozen will be mapped out in the Valdichiana Active sustainable-tourism network.

Back in San Casciano, follow 'Terme acqua calda' signs to the Roman trio of free, travertine-stone basins still in use at the foot of the hilltop village. Bathing in the hot water (around 40°C/104°F) is magical after dark, as the moonlight and twinkling stars plunge you into ancient Tuscany's extraordinary resurrected soul.

1 The 16th-century church of San Biagio outside Montepulciano 2 Siena's Duomo is a Gothic masterpiece 3 Piazza Grande in Arezzo 4 Tuscany's prized Chianina breed 5 An ancient Etruscan bronze unearthed at San Casciano dei Bagni 6 Siena's skyline would still be familiar to Renaissance painters

Getting there

By plane or train to Pisa or Florence, then car or bus/train to Siena/Arezzo and e-bike into the rural valley. Tiemme (tiemmespa. it) operates bus routes, and several bicycle-rental outlets in Siena have e-bikes.

When to go

May, June, September and October promise pleasantly warm temperatures, fewer crowds and walking trails spangled with wild flowers.

Further reading

Sybille Haynes' *Etruscan Civilisation: A Cultural History* is precisely that. In *The Etruscan* by Mika Wiltari, a young man travels from Greece to Tuscany in 480 BCE, in search of the meaning of life.

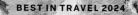

DONEGAL, IRELAND

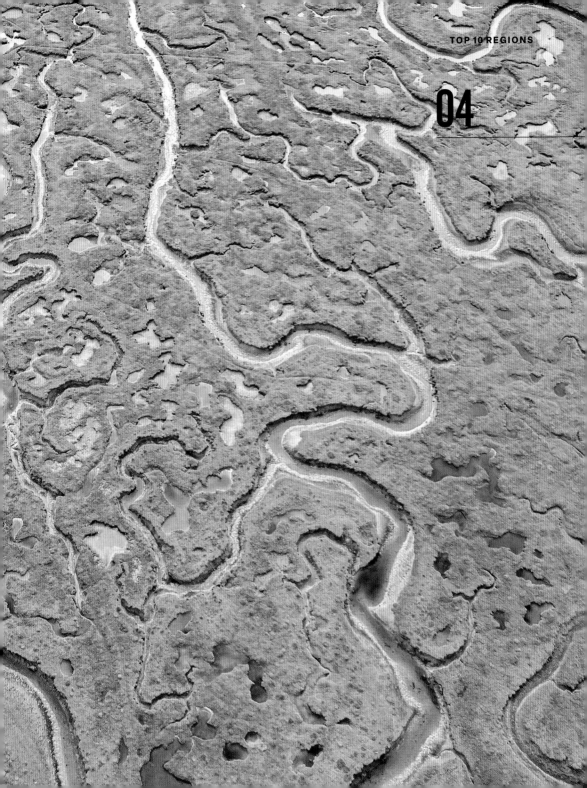

W ith the longest coastline in Ireland and more than 100 beaches, Donegal makes it possible to find yourself the only person on a deserted strand. Slightly off radar, the northernmost Irish county does wildness but with a big heart and a neighbourly feel. Here you'll find the highest sea cliffs in Europe at Sliabh Liag, at 601m (1972ft), and miles of unspoilt coastal hiking trails along the Wild Atlantic Way. Its ancient forts, musical traditions and rich heritage of the Irish language also make it an immersive experience for the curious visitor.

1 Lukasek/Shutterstock © 2 Simon Gray/500px ©

Highlights

01 **Dubbed the best-kept secret** on the Wild Atlantic Way, Ireland's highest sea cliffs at Sliabh Liag (Slieve League) are jaw-droppingly beautiful. They are also the highest accessible sea cliffs in Europe, dwarfing the Eiffel Tower and the more touristy Cliffs of Moher.

02 **Don't miss** a chance for a dip at the beautiful Silver Strand, a horseshoe-shaped cove near Malin Beg outside Glencolmcille.

03 **No visit to Donegal** is complete without a trip to Ireland's most northerly point, Malin Head, a rocky cape where the northern lights may sometimes be seen.

3 Lukasek/Shutterstock ©

Otherworldly beaches and unparalleled hikes

Donegal's magnificent beaches are undoubtedly its best-kept secret, and you're never far from a magical swim spot. From the blushing sands of Ballymastocker Bay on the western shores of Lough Swilly, to the sweeping descent to rugged and well-concealed Kinnagoe Bay in Inishowen, the pull of the ocean is unrivalled, and you might be the only person for miles around.

With trees growing right to the water's edge, Ards Forest Park is full of deserted coves perfect for a dip - especially if you find the aptly-named sands of Lucky Shell Beach - before browsing the shops in the pretty seaside town of Dunfanaghy a short drive away. For the more adventurous, the wild expanse of Glenveagh National Park is full of hiking trails, and a new pathway is becoming a major draw to the tip of the county, where the mountain peak of Errigal stands proudly in the Donegal Highlands.

Get active

Donegal has one of Ireland's largest collections of activity tourism businesses, often family run. Many operators have been focusing on slow and sustainable tourism, and their efforts are starting to pay off. Hugh Hunter's Eco Atlantic Adventures takes visitors on kayaking tours of Lough Swilly with an emphasis on keeping costs and mileage to and from tour sites low.

Cycling doesn't have to be a downhill adrenaline rush; Off The Beaten Path runs slow

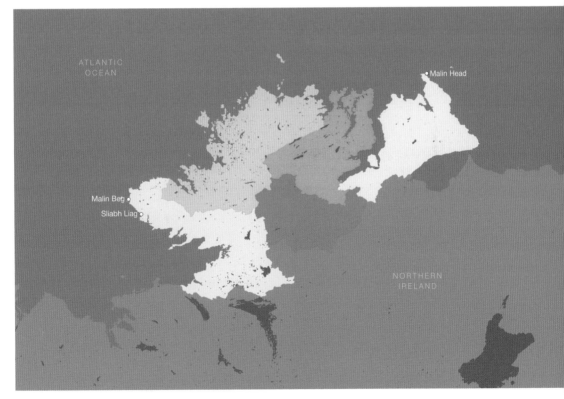

I love walking on Fintra Beach or watching the fishing boats come into Killybegs with their heavy loads. Killybegs is where you come to get away from it all and just breathe.

Mairead O'Hagan Anderson, who with her husband runs the Seafood Shack and Anderson's Boathouse Restaurant and accommodation in the fishing town of Killybegs

and scenic electric 'fat bike' tours of Glenveagh National Park, rides that hug the coast around Magheraroarty, and circuits of Tory Island.

The magnificent sea-stack-spotted coastline off Arranmore Island is an unforgettable Donegal experience. The two-hour sea safari and maritime heritage tours that leave from the island run at a pace that is respectful to local wildlife, including seals, dolphins and their young. The island is also introducing a snorkel trail for beginners and more experienced snorkellers.

And if you're going to be in the spiritual home of Irish surfing, you've got to take to the waves. Fin McCool Surf School is located only footsteps from the wide expanse of Rossnowlagh Beach.

Neighbourhood food

From pop-ups to award-winning chefs who've moved back home to Donegal for work/life balance, the county is brimming with buzz about new eateries opened up since the pandemic, with a focus on local produce and affordability with a homespun feel.

Since he took over the kitchen at the Olde Glen Bar near Carrigart, head chef Ciarán Sweeney started a food revolution, prompting chefs in the county to raise their game. Making use of local oysters and fish off the boat several times a day, he has a renewed focus on unfussy but sharp food that's won a place in the Michelin guide. From Fisk Seafood Bar in Downings to Nancy's Barn bistro in Ballyliffin on the Inishowen Peninsula, chefs are cooking what's in season and available locally, like Nancy's award-winning seafood chowder served with wheaten bread.

1 Riverside marshes at Ards Forest Park 2 Round-leaved sundews are a staple of Ireland's bogs 3 The lighthouse at Fanad Head 4 A church in Dunlewey on the slopes of Errigal 5 Cycling above Lough Beagh in Glenveagh National Park 6 Malin Beg's Silver Strand

Getting there

By car, Belfast City and Belfast International airports are a 2hr drive from Donegal's coast; Dublin's airport is a 3hr drive away. There are also bus links from major towns and cities.

When to go

The summer months are busier with visitors, but winter offers opportunities for watching migratory birds. The Earagail Arts Festival in July celebrates local culture and language.

Further reading

Cathal Coyle's *The Little Book of Donegal* is a pocket-size guide to folklore and customs, while Sean Beattie and Jim MacLaughlin's *An Historical, Environmental and Cultural Atlas of County Donegal* is the ultimate guide.

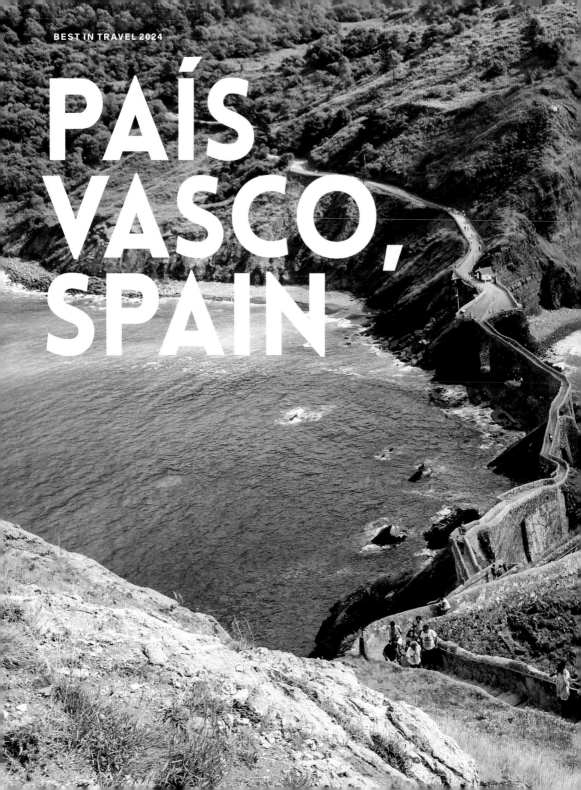

PAÍS VASCO, SPAIN

05

Bordering southwest France on Spain's surf-washed north coast, the País Vasco (called Euskadi by the Basques) is a wildly beautiful, endlessly captivating place. The unmatched local gastronomy sets the scene for this region's rich, unique and ancient culture, along with Euskara (the Basque language), a whirl of distinctive fiestas and more. This is the birthplace of Spain's *cocina alta* (high cuisine), and you'll feel it in the fired-up food scenes of post-industrial Bilbao, elegant San Sebastián and buzzy Vitoria-Gasteiz, where fresh art-world ventures are blossoming, too. The entire region is pushing forward initiatives to develop more sustainable, positive-impact tourism, and a high-speed AVE train line is also in the works.

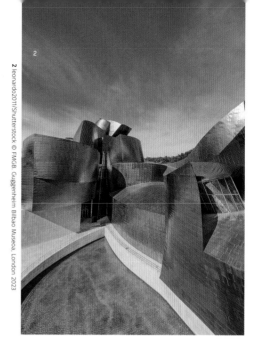

2 leonardo2011/Shutterstock © FMGB Guggenheim Bilbao Museoa, London 2023

Highlights

01 **Dive into San Sebastián's** gastronomy, from *pintxo* bars (Casa Urola, Borda Berri, Bergara, Tamboril) to a wine tour (mimo.eus).

02 **Catching the legendary left-hand wave** at Mundaka is a dream for experienced surfers. Zarautz and Sopelana are other top spots.

03 **Soak up Bilbao's** open-air sculptures and murals on a stroll along the Nervión, or join a bike tour with Tourné (tournebilbao.com).

04 **Hike the rugged peaks** of Anboto and Aizkorri, or coastal routes such as the cliff-hugging trail from San Sebastián to Pasaia.

1 Daliusposus/Shutterstock © 3 Justin Folkes/Lonely Planet ©

Glorious Basque gastronomy

The País Vasco is undoubtedly one of the world's greatest places to eat, home to four of Spain's 13 triple-Michelin-starred restaurants. Life-changing meals await around every corner, from the humble *pintxo* morsel (elevated to an art in San Sebastián, Bilbao and beyond) to the creative culinary wizardry of chefs like Martín Berasategui (currently the Spanish chef with most Michelin stars), Bittor Arginzoniz (of Asador Etxebarri fame) and Juan Mari Arzak and Elena Arzak (the father-daughter duo behind Arzak). All over the region, top chefs continue to innovate and inspire, while keeping their craft rooted in the freshest local produce and celebrating traditional recipes passed down through generations.

But it isn't all Michelin stars. Basque dining is just as much about savouring cider and traditional-style menus of cod omelette and sizzling steak in a down-to-earth *sagardotegi* (ciderhouse); feasting on fresh seafood overlooking the Bay of Biscay; sipping a crisp Txakoli in a chic wine bar; or exploring cutting-edge *bodegas* in the Rioja Alavesa wine region.

Urban thrills

In stylish San Sebastián, fresh-faced hotels and new galleries such as Villa Magdalena are making a splash among the gold-hued beaches and belle époque architecture, while the surf-loving Gros neighbourhood grows cooler every year. It's a similar scene over in dynamic Bilbao, where the

Basque cuisine is a cuisine of sensibility, with local roots, of great produce, both contemporary and investigative. And all within a sustainable ethos. Akelarre, for example, is marvellous for its restaurants and hotel, or try Ganbara for pintxos in San Sebastián.

Elena Arzak, joint head chef at three-Michelin-star restaurant Arzak, San Sebastián

arts continue to thrive, from the unmissable Frank Gehry-designed Guggenheim to revitalised Zorrotzaurre island (originally conceived by Zaha Hadid), the industrial buildings being reborn as cultural spaces. Art-deco Mercado de la Ribera remains one of Spain's great produce markets, and there are fabulous *pintxo* spots all over the place, like Gure Toki on the Casco Viejo's Plaza Nueva or La Viña del Ensanche across the river. The País Vasco's inland capital Vitoria-Gasteiz is a less-touristed delight with its own wonderful world of *pintxos*, a lively street-art scene and superb galleries such as Artium.

The Basque coast
All along the coastline, jade-coloured fields give way to windswept cliffs on the Bay of Biscay. The region was a pioneer for surfing in Spain back in the 1960s and today its entire coast is a surfers' haven, from San Sebastián's urban beaches to

fabled Mundaka, with its colourful fishing port on the Urdaibai estuary near Gernika. Other rewarding coastal stops include Lekeitio (home to magical Isla de Garraitz, accessible only at low tide), Getaria (birthplace of designer Cristóbal Balenciaga) and the spectacular islet and 10th-century chapel of San Juan de Gaztelugatxe (which *Game of Thrones* fans will recognise as Dragonstone). Meanwhile, the less-travelled inland reaches are dominated by rolling farmlands where stone-built villages dot the landscape, and walking trails weave into the hills.

1 The narrow causeway to San Juan de Gaztelugatxe
2 Bilbao's game-changing Guggenheim **3** Playa de La Concha in San Sebastián **4** *Pintxos* have become ever more inventive **5** The mythological figure of Basajaun at a parade in Bilbao **6** The fishing port of Bermeo, near Mundaka

Getting there
Bilbao, San Sebastián and Biarritz (just over the border in France) are handy airports for arriving in the País Vasco. Bilbao, San Sebastián and Vitoria-Gasteiz all have good train links with the centre of Spain.

When to go
The warm summer months (July and August) are peak season on the coast, especially in San Sebastián; this is also when many festivals happen (such as Bilbao's nine-day Aste Nagusia) and a great time for hiking in the mountains. June and September can be quieter but still warm. Spring and autumn are ideal for both hiking and surfing, while the Tamborrada drum festival brings winter fun to San Sebastián in mid-January.

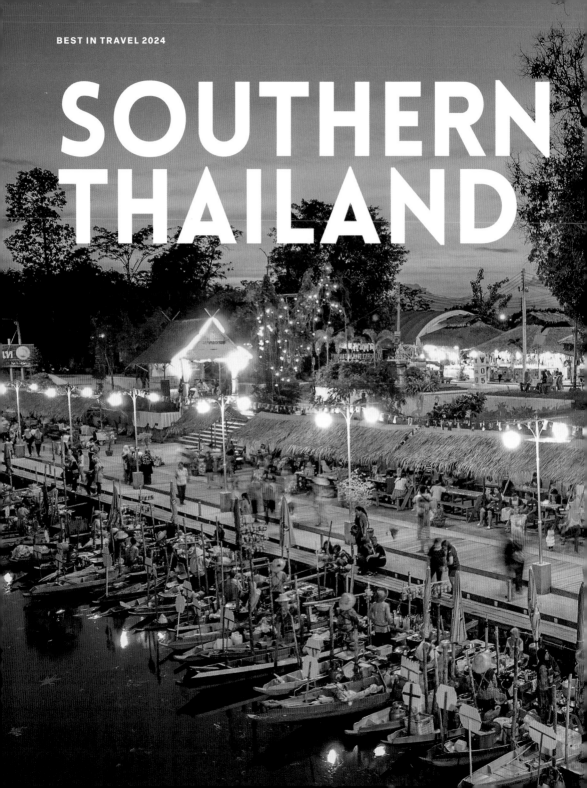

SOUTHERN THAILAND

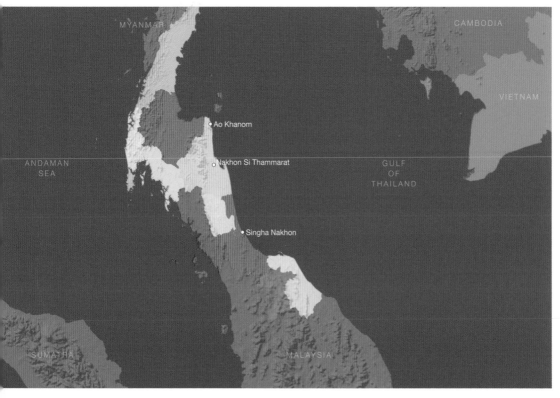

MYANMAR

CAMBODIA

VIETNAM

Ao Khanom

ANDAMAN
SEA

Nakhon Si Thammarat

GULF
OF
THAILAND

Singha Nakhon

SUMATRA

MALAYSIA

W elcome to another Thailand:
a Thailand of ornate mosques
and mystical shrines, where the
melodious call to prayer chimes
with the sound of temple bells; where a
distinct halal cuisine and a unique local culture
has emerged from centuries of Thai, Malay and
Indo-Persian cross-pollination. Welcome to
Muslim Thailand. This is a place that celebrates
a rich and fascinating history stretching back
several centuries, with tales of miraculous
saints and all-conquering sultans; a region
that is also home to miles of deserted beaches,
traditional fishing villages and stunning,
jungle-cloaked national parks.

1 eakkachai/Shutterstock © 2 Tharik Hussain © 3 anamachat/Shutterstock ©

Thai-Islam

Mainland southern Thailand *is* Muslim Thailand; the spiritual home of the country's second-largest, and oft-marginalised, religious community. This is the Thailand you rarely read about, and if you do it is almost always reduced to little more than tales of troublesome insurgents; but look beyond the popular headlines and a world of spectacularly eclectic and unique mosque architecture, delightful food and colourful festivals awaits.

The further south you go, the more you'll notice a pronounced shift in the culture and people here; things begin to increasingly resemble life across the border in Malaysia, with the region drawing on a fascinating heritage rich in Persian, Arab and Indo-Asian influence.

This is an area with ornate shrines dedicated to miracle-performing Sufi saints, revered by Buddhists and Muslims alike; where on special holy nights the hypnotic chanting of devotees fills the air, and the call to prayer emanates five times a day from mosques with an architectural style that marries the traditional Thai with the classical Islamic.

Forgotten sultanates

Once ruled by sultans and Muslim queens, whose domains traded with the colonial powers of Europe and even stood up to the might of historic Thai empires in the north, the south's fabulous Islamic history has now been largely forgotten. Yet curious travellers can head into the jungle-covered hills of places like Singha

Highlights

01 **Join an open iftar** – visit in Ramadan to experience the warmth of communally breaking fast with southern Thai-Muslim food.

02 **Wander through untamed jungle** in Singha Nakhon in search of the ruins of the forgotten Sultanate of Singora.

03 **Eat your way** through Nakhon Si Thammarat's nocturnal food market, which brims with delicious local Muslim dishes.

04 **Lie on a deserted beach** near Ao Khanom, and wait to glimpse elusive and beautiful pink dolphins.

Nakhon in search of ruins of ancient kingdoms like the Sultanate of Singora; pulling back thick vines to reveal its forgotten city walls and near-complete military forts, where rusting cannons still point out to sea.

Then there is the deeper south; still a place of conflict but also the heart of historic Muslim Thailand, which preserves the country's oldest and most symbolic Islamic monument, the 16th-century Krue-Se Mosque near Pattani. It has distinct Persian architecture, and stands as a reminder of the region's Golden Age.

Quieter Thailand

Overlooked by tourists, the south is also home to some of the most isolated stretches of coastline in the country. Rock up at places like Ao Khanom and you'll have an entire beach all to yourself, with no one but the odd shy pink dolphin for company; hop onto a moped and trace the quiet coastal paths as they meander through out-of-the-way fishing villages where dozing fisherfolk looking out to the azure sea from the steps of small mosques; pause at a local tea hut where women in patterned hijabs welcome you with fresh *má·tà·bà* and *chah* (stuffed roti and tea), a meal every Arab and Indian knows well.

Blessed with a host of authentic Thai cities such as Nakhon Si Thammarat, Surat Thani and Hat Yai, the southern provinces, like much

When in Songkhla, you have to have 'egg yolk ice cream' from Yew Ice Cream Shop, it's unique in Thailand!

Abdu'r Rahman, owner of Ban Nai Nakhon Boutique Hotel, Songkhla

of Thailand, are also highly accessible for independent travellers; trains, buses, microvans and ferries will take you to every corner of the region, whether it is to go in search of clouded leopards in the lush, green mountain surrounds of Khao Luang National Park, or to admire the gorgeous Sino-Portuguese architecture in the Old Town of Songkhla.

When you think of the south, think of Thailand before the backpackers: quiet, cheap and with the added bonus of a spectacular Thai-Muslim culture.

1 Khlong Hae Floating Market, Hat Yai **2** A cannon inside a historic Muslim fort **3** Hat Yai street-food **4** The Central Mosque between Songkhla and Hat Yai **5** Ruins of Singora's city walls, Songkhla Province **6** Coastal rice paddies near Nakhon Si Thammarat

Getting there

There are regional flights, trains and coaches from Bangkok to all the hub cities in the south, and ferries from most of the popular islands.

When to go

July to October is monsoon season. In 2024, Ramadan falls across March and April, and Eid-ul-adha is in the middle of June. Always seek out up-to-date guidance – international travel warnings advise against visiting the four southernmost Thai provinces.

Further reading

Start with *The Muslims of Thailand* by Michael Gilquin; and *Muslim Worship Sites in Thailand* by Suthep Sudwilai.

07

SWAHILI COAST, TANZANIA

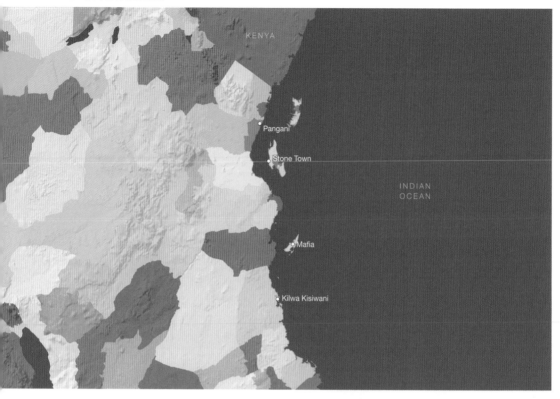

Tanzania's Swahili Coast has been welcoming travellers for millennia. Early visitors arrived on monsoon-driven trade routes that extended to Arabia, India and China, and shaped local culture. Today, past and present are inextricably intertwined. Moss-covered ruins are flanked by modern hotels. Fishermen in wooden *ngalawa* paddle in the shadow of high-speed ferries. Vendors hawk cashews on street corners while, metres away, mega business deals are made in gleaming, high-rise office blocks. There has never been a better time to explore than now, as the region looks confidently to the future under the leadership of Tanzania's first female president.

Local rhythms

Once you arrive, immerse yourself in local rhythms. Paddle along sultry, mangrove-lined channels on Mafia Island or visit sun-baked villages where life goes on as it has for centuries. Explore the remains of a 700-year-old palace on Kilwa Kisiwani. Marvel at centuries-old Chinese pottery shards that wash up occasionally on the beach. Wander through the winding alleyways of Zanzibar's Stone Town, with its carved doorways and houses built of crumbling coral stone, or take a sunset cruise on a dhow, its white canvas sails billowing in the breeze. Luxuriate for a night or a few in comfortable island lodges, appreciating the warm welcome of local guesthouses, dining on subtly spiced coastal cuisine and nibbling on grilled *pweza* (octopus) at lively, candle-lit night markets. The more you delve into the past, the more you will get to know modern-day Tanzania and Tanzanians.

Coastal vibes

Swim with whale sharks on Mafia Island and learn about local marine conservation. Listen to *taarab* music on Zanzibar. Explore hidden coves and see cloves drying in the sun on Pemba. In tiny Saadani National Park, watch as elephants walk along the sand and flamingos gather by the river delta, or head to Nyerere National Park – the region's flagship protected area – and let expert guides take you past shallow lakes and stands of borassus palms to

Highlights

01 **Transport yourself back in time** at the World Heritage Site of Kilwa Kisiwani, once the seat of a far-flung trading empire.

02 **Dine on fragrant pilau** or coconut curry at one of the many wonderful restaurants in Zanzibar's old Stone Town.

03 **Spend time on Mafia,** overnighting in one of the island's eco-conscious lodges and enjoying the tranquil pace.

04 **Snorkel around** a pristine sandbank or stroll along palm-shaded beaches near the old Swahili trading settlement of Pangani.

Getting there

Ferries and planes connect the coast with the islands, while dhows or small outriggers will take you across narrower channels.

When to go

The rains are heaviest from mid-March to May, when some park- and island-based lodges close for several weeks, but greenery, flowers and birds abound. Wildlife-watching is at its prime from June to October.

Further reading

In *Paradise*, Zanzibar-born Nobel Prize winner Abdulrazak Gurnah explores the impact of colonialism and migration, while Elieshi Lema's *Parched Earth* reflects on modern-day womanhood through a woman's eyes.

show you where a lion has just passed while stalking its prey. Relish the opportunity to float along the wide Rufiji River on a boat safari, while your captain navigates around hippos submerged in the shallows, glides near crocodiles sunning themselves on the rocks, and points out kingfishers near the steep riverbanks.

Looking to the future

The Swahili Coast's roots are long and its branches far-reaching; its people are comfortable with who they are and where they have come from, proud of the present and full of ideas for the future. In Dar es Salaam, the region's athletes are setting their sights on international competitions. More students than ever are striving for further education, as enrollment numbers increase and universities are stretched

I love living in Tanzania because it's my country of birth. It's a young nation and so much is happening. The new leadership is embracing many exciting opportunities. Yet, throughout, we Tanzanians remain very humble people.

Simon Mtuy, athlete and passionate developer of adventure sports

to capacity. Amidst all this, the government is steadily steering its path and the economy is growing. The enterprising vendors who work the streets are selling much more than just cashews. Late for a business meeting and forgot your dress shirt? You'll be able to find one kerbside, at the next junction. Energies are high, and the mood is upbeat. There's never been a better time than now to get acquainted with Tanzania's Swahili Coast and meet its people. *Jambo*, hello, and *karibu*, welcome.

1 The shores of Zanzibar have been plied by traders for centuries **2** Beaded ornaments for sale in a Zanzibar market **3** Delivering bread through the streets of Stone Town **4** End of the day on historic Songo Mnara island **5** Walking on a Zanzibar beach **6** Whale sharks swim in the waters off Mafia Island

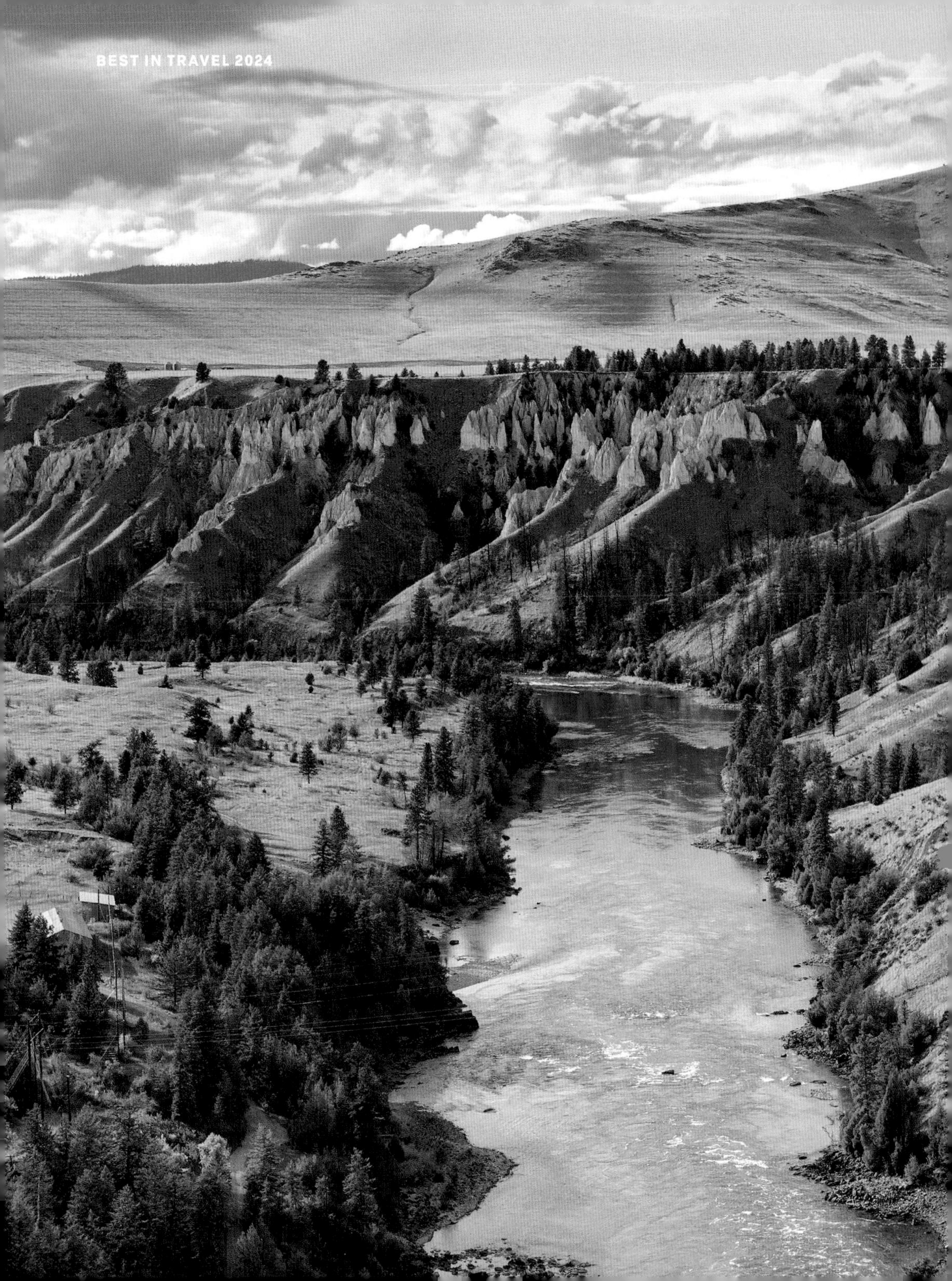

08

MONTANA, USA

W ith public lands covering around 121,400 sq km (46,873 sq miles), some of the most majestic scenery in the US (ever-more film-makers are catching on), and a growing emphasis on culture, food and drink, Montana is a destination for everyone from outdoor adventurers to families looking for a peaceful getaway close to nature. Whether you're aiming for backcountry miles in the wilderness, seeking the rich history of Native culture in the region, or you prefer to stay in the mountain-town hubs of Bozeman and Missoula, Montana has something for everyone, any season.

Escape to the wild

Glacier National Park (traditional lands of the Blackfeet, Salish, Pend d'Oreille and Kootenai)

1 Justin Foulkes/Lonely Planet © 2 urbancow/Getty Images ©

Highlights

01 **Skiing and hot springs** are top Montana draws. Do both in a day at Showdown and at White Sulphur Springs' Hot Springs Motel.

02 **Take a tour** with Sun Tours' experienced Blackfeet Guides to explore the ancestral culture and history of Glacier National Park.

03 **Get your ice-cream fix** at Big Dipper: with branches in Helena, Billings and Missoula, it's garnered national attention.

04 **Explore a real mine** at Butte's World Museum of Mining, where film-worthy buildings are packed with 1800s artefacts.

3 EB Adventure Photography/Shutterstock ©

and Yellowstone National Park (traditional lands of the Kiowa, Blackfeet, Cayuse, Coeur d'Alene, Shoshone and Nez Perce) are huge tourism drivers in the state, and for good reason. They are bucket-list national parks, which means they tend to get packed during the summer. If you're looking for similar views without the crowds, try exploring one of the 15 wilderness areas in Montana, including heavy-hitters like the Bob Marshall Wilderness (traditional lands of the Blackfeet, Salish and Kootenai) or the Absaroka-Beartooth Wilderness (traditional lands of the Apsáalooke). Some trails throughout these areas are believed to be remnants of the original corridors of Indigenous peoples, marking history with every footstep.

Wilderness areas are one of the easiest public-land designations to access, and 2024 is no different. While some areas require permits, most are still self-serve at the trailhead, and it's up to each visitor to explore responsibly and safely while enjoying the jaw-dropping scenery.

Scenic backdrops

From period westerns to modern dramas, Montana's film industry is booming. 2024 will see

1 Flathead River rock pinnacles, downstream from Polson **2** Fishing at Parade Rest Guest Ranch near Yellowstone **3** Kayaking Lake McDonald, Glacier National Park **4** Yellowstone bull elk **5** Butte's World Museum of Mining **6** Avalanche Lake, Glacier NP

Living in Montana isn't just about the amazing outdoor spaces and recreational opportunities... It's about the people who will help you in a crisis, the appreciation we have for our ecosystems, and the nonprofits working to ensure their continuation. Everywhere you look, Montana encourages looking after the places you put your feet and the people you walk beside. It's a wonderful place to live.

Laryssa Rote, Helena-based adventure cyclist and wildlife rehabilitator

the release of numerous big-screen movies, indie flicks and television shows shot in Montana. From the jagged peaks surrounding Paradise Valley to the rolling hills outside Missoula, a trip to Montana means experiencing the real-life movie locations for yourself.

Paramount's runaway hit *Yellowstone* is filmed mostly in the rugged country around Missoula, and many in-town scenes for the prequel *1923* are filmed right in downtown Butte. Over the last four years, numerous indie films have been shot at the Yellowstone Film Ranch outside Livingston, all with the towering Emigrant Peak in the background.

Big-town amenities, small-town charm

The influx of people looking to escape cities during the pandemic helped build up Montana's mountain towns, many of which are close to ski resorts, hot springs, cultural sites with historical Native significance and national parks. While many visit Montana for backcountry adventures, the in-town experience is reason enough. From locally roasted coffee to dozens of breweries and farm-to-table restaurants, Montana's mountain-town culture has been expanding, bringing in world-class chefs to the food scenes of Missoula, Whitefish, Big Sky, Bozeman and Helena.

Each of these towns saw many new restaurants opening in the past year, and they all have a vibrant brewery scene. For those on a brewery tour, hit up Highlander Beer in Missoula, Lewis and Clark Brewing Co in Helena, Bridger Brewing in Bozeman, and Blackstar in Whitefish.

Getting there
Larger airports include Bozeman, Billings, Missoula, Great Falls and Kalispell. Renting a car once you arrive isn't a bad idea, as public transport is minimal in most places.

When to go
Montana is a four-season wonderland, with rafting in the summer, hiking in the autumn, fly fishing in spring, and skiing in winter. Be aware that snow that can stretch into May, and late summer may see wildfire smoke.

Further reading
Norman Maclean's *A River Runs Through It* is a classic; C Thomas Shay's *Under Prairie Skies: The Plants and Native Peoples of the Northern Plains* offers a dive into Indigenous culture.

SAALFELDEN LEOGANG, AUSTRIA

09

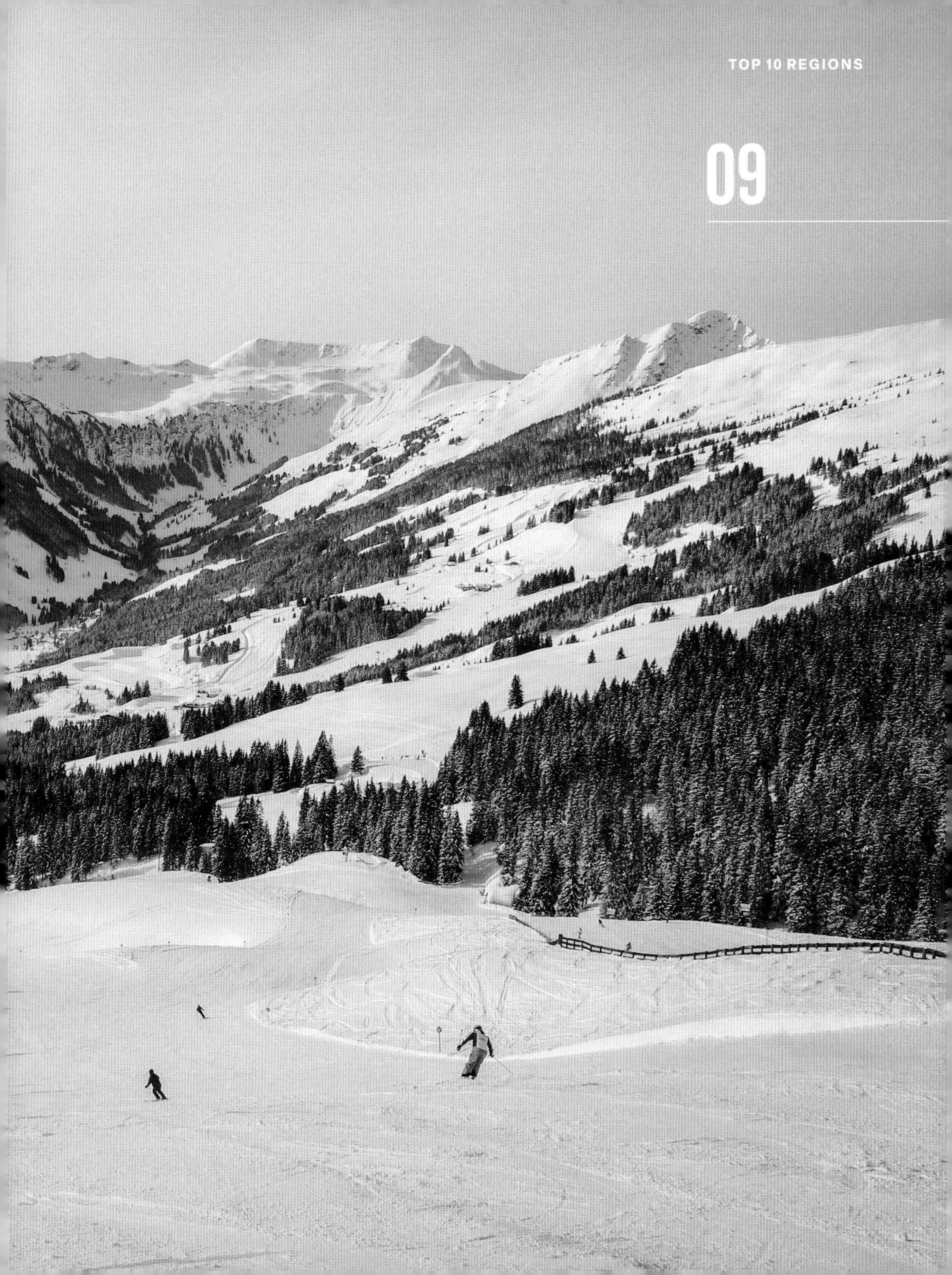

Whether you're watching a fiery sunset blaze across limestone peaks, bolting through pine woods in one of Europe's most thrilling MTB parks, listening to a mountaintop Bach concert or snowshoeing through fresh powder, nature is writ large in Saalfelden Leogang. In 2024, this mountain resort in Austria's Salzburgerland region is making its way to a more sustainable future, with a new green chairlift, an insanely stylish spa, and a flurry of guided outdoor activities throwing you in right at the Alpine deep end.

Most folk blaze past Saalfelden Leogang without so much as a passing nod in the mad dash to Salzburg, just north, or glitzy Kitzbühel, just west.

1 Krystof Guth/Shutterstock © 2 Ulrich Hoschek/Shutterstock ©

3 Eder/Shutterstock ©

Highlights

01 **Hire an e-bike** for a food-loving spin, with highlights including the Wölfler family's saffron-growing farm, and HPH anno 1905 shop.

02 **Zip across the valley** at speeds of up to 130km/h (80mph) on the Flying Fox XXL at Asitz, perhaps the closest you'll get to flight.

03 **Slip back to nature** in the new lakeside Krallerhof Atmosphere Spa, flowing seamlessly into the mountain landscape.

04 **Hike to high pastures** and the rustic Lindlalm hut, where Resi cooks faves like *Pinzgauer Kasnock'n* (cheesy mini-dumplings).

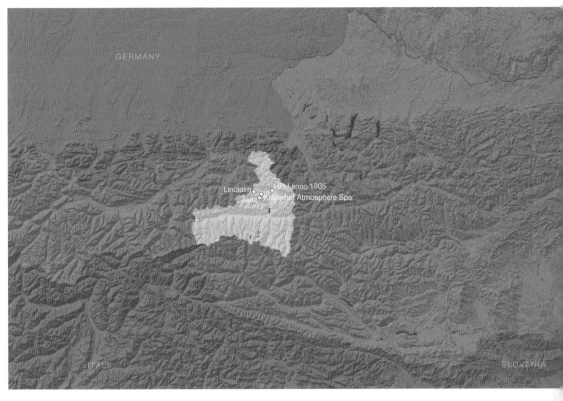

But they are missing a secret. Why? The Leogang Steinberge Mountains tower above wildflower-freckled valleys and lakes of stained-glass blue. Nearby, where Austria bumps into Germany, the limestone peaks of the Steinernes Meer are raised up like a theatre curtain above a vast karst plateau beloved of hikers and climbers.

In 2024, the spotlight turns on Saalfelden Leogang's phenomenal backyard and impeccable eco credentials. With a growing crop of MTB trails twisting deep into forests rich in wildlife, a slick new eight-seater chairlift with solar panels providing green energy, and an architecturally striking lakefront spa echoing the beauty of the surrounding lakes and mountains, the resort is finally getting its moment to shine.

Elevating art

Hovering around the 1900m (6234ft) mark, Asitz has dress-circle views of a pair of sparkling lakes and ragged peaks punching above Alpine valleys. It's dubbed the 'Mountain of Senses' and you can believe the hype. In summer, its pine forests double as exhibition walls for a one-of-a-kind art trail, and folk, rock and classical music bounces off the peaks at the open-air TONspuren concerts (the acoustics are excellent).

Year-round you'll find installations designed to make you reflect, relax and press the reset button. Cue the Cinema of Nature – lookouts where you can swoon over knockout views of the mountains from a hammock or reclining wooden chair – and scenically perched TONspur

4 Ilan Shacham/Getty Images © 5 Martin Erdniss/Shutterstock © 6 Nyokki/Shutterstock ©

My favourite panoramic bike tour is the Steinalm plateau in Saalfelden, with surround views of the three different mountain ranges (limestone, slate and the Hohe Tauern) and the basin and river of Saalfelden Leogang. It leaves no nature lover untouched.

Sabine Enzinger, bike and offpiste guide and founder of Elements Outdoor Sports

huts, where you can peak-gaze while listening to concert recordings.

Moving mountains

One glance at these heights and you'll be itching to ski, ride, hike and climb. Mountain bikers are in their element at the Epic Bike Park, spread across seven peaks. The terrain is vast, views are epic, and technically demanding passages, north shores and root areas will leave you buzzing.

Prefer to walk? Hook onto the Climate Hike, whisking you through time in the tracks of ice and water, or ramp up the challenge on the long-distance, 68km (42-mile) Saalachtaler Höhenweg, with spirit-lifting views of Austria's highest peaks in the Hohe Tauern National Park. Pole-sharing stations and vending machines with organic farm produce make hoofing it a pleasure. And if you would prefer some company, the tourist office has just launched a year-round programme

of guided activities from ski tours to wildlife-spotting rambles and herb workshops, many of which are free with your guest card.

With the first dusting of snow and waxing of skis, Saalfelden Leogang is the full-on winter dream. The Skicircus has 270km (168 miles) of downhill runs to carve, but as the resort speeds towards sustainability, it's paving the way for a cleaner, greener future by embracing lower-impact, nature-focused activities like ski touring, snowshoeing, winter hiking and cross-country skiing on 150km (93 miles) of groomed trails.

1 A blue run above Hinterglemm, part of the Skicircus area shared with Leogang and Saalbach **2** Reaching for the skies **3** Skyline rides at the top of Asitz **4** Leogang's bike trails cover some 80km (50 miles) **5** A lakeside rest stop near Asitz' summit **6** A chapel in Au, north of Saalfelden

Getting there

Get off to a green start by arriving on the winter-only overnight Alpen Express, which returned in 2022 and links the Netherlands (and its Eurostar connections) with Saalfelden. Otherwise, Saalfelden is under 2hr by train from both Salzburg and Innsbruck, with flight connections across Europe, especially in winter-sports season.

When to go

Winter is all about the snow, while summer ramps up the cultural and outdoor action with TONspuren concerts, art trails and peak-gazing at the summit of Asitz, UCI Mountain Bike World Cup events, and a feast of hiking and biking. Shoulder seasons often see hotels closed for a breather.

FAR NORTH SCOTLAND

10

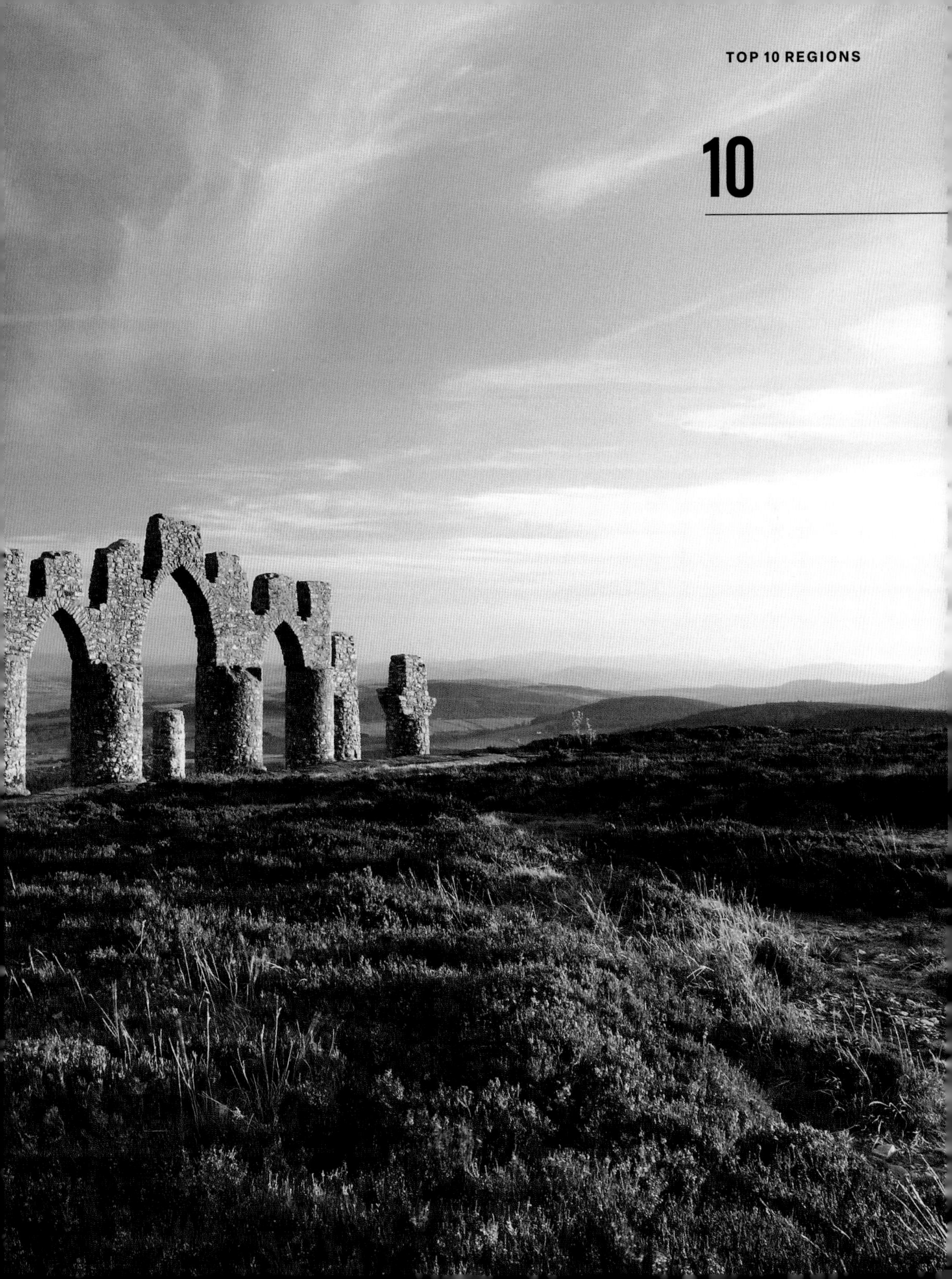

Crowds in Scotland instinctively flow to the battlements of Edinburgh Castle, the shores of Loch Lomond and the peaks of Glencoe. A relative trickle of travellers heads northward to the Flow Country: a watery expanse hidden beyond the Highlands' loftiest ranges. Nonetheless, 2024 will hopefully mean new recognition for this region, as it aims to achieve Unesco World Heritage status. Now's the perfect time to make a trip to the far north of Scotland, exploring both its unsung boggy interior and a coastline of heartbreaking beauty.

Go with the flow

Up on the roof of Scotland is the evocatively named Flow Country, one of Europe's most bleakly beautiful ecosystems. It counts among the most

1 Birson Calfort/Shutterstock © 2 365_visuals/Shutterstock ©

3 Helen Hotson/Shutterstock ©

Highlights

01 **Make an ascent** of Ben Hope, Scotland's northernmost Munro (a peak over 914m/3000ft), with sweeping Flow Country views.

02 **Explore ornate Dunrobin Castle,** among the largest houses in Scotland, and discover its dark role in the Highland Clearances.

03 **Drive the spectacular** section of the North Coast 500 south of Durness, crossing the magnificent Kylesku Bridge.

04 **Go birdwatching** in the Forsinard Flows Nature Reserve, visited by species including golden plovers and hen harriers.

sparsely populated regions of the entire continent, a place almost as far from the English border as it is from the Norwegian fjords. And it was, indeed, the Vikings that gave the region its name. 'Flow' comes from the Old Norse word for 'wet', and some 3885 sq km (1500 sq miles) of blanket bog are defined by an intricate interplay of land and water, with peatlands carved by a maze of mirror-like channels that sparkle on long summer evenings, and ice over on long winter nights. If, in 2024, it's space for silence and contemplation you're seeking, this could be the place for you.

This year will also see the Flow Country contending for Unesco World Heritage status – for not only is this ecosystem rich in rare flora and fauna, but it also stands on the frontline of the climate crisis, with the peat serving as a vast sink for carbon that would otherwise enter the Earth's atmosphere. The boggy terrain is often treacherous and impassable on foot; fortunately a wooden walkway winds through the RSPB's Forsinard Flows Nature Reserve to the Flows Lookout. From this strikingly designed tower you might spot dippers and dunlins, greenshank and golden plover swooping about the clear horizons.

1 The Fyrish Monument, built during the Highland Clearances **2** Highland cattle can withstand the elements **3** Kylesku Bridge on the North Coast 500 **4** Duncansby Stacks near John O'Groats **5** Fishing gear in Helmsdale **6** The faces of Dunrobin Castle

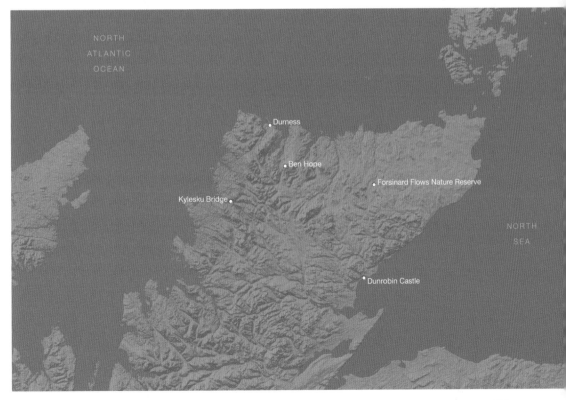

The Flow Country is an enigmatic landscape – a place of sweeping moorlands and bogs that's quite hard to appreciate on a first visit. You need to spend a bit of time walking here, a bit of time sitting down too. I find the longer it takes to get to know a place, the deeper your understanding.

Dr Steven Andrews, Flow Country World Heritage Project

Ocean drives

If saltwater is more your thing, the coastline on the Flow Country's fringes is also enthralling, skirted by the popular North Coast 500 motoring route. Dornoch is a handsome cathedral town backed by a sweep of golden sand, while to the north lies the fishing village of Helmsdale, enclosed by a huddle of gorse-blanketed hills. Pressing onward, you enter lighthouse country: from the light at Dunnet Head - mainland Britain's northernmost point - to its storm-lashed sibling at Cape Wrath in the west, a sequence of whitewashed towers cast blinking lights out into the swells. It's a coastline often seen through a car windscreen, but there are ample opportunities to get out and feel the elements. Thurso is the surfing capital of Scotland, with peak conditions coinciding with the darkest depths of winter; fortunately it's possible to

arrange surf lessons with (thick) wetsuits, and warm up with a dram of whisky soon afterwards.

Time out

Food and drink is getting ever more attention in these parts - the shellfish plucked from the sea lochs of the northwestern coast is legendary. More than likely, Atlantic weather will at some point chase you indoors, to the snug of a cafe, tearoom or bar, to a hot meal and quite possibly into the company of locals too. But in truth, the appeal of this nook of Scotland for many travellers lies in moments of profound solitude. Dotted around are Neolithic burial chambers, and abandoned crofters' cottages dating to the Highland Clearances - places where the ghosts of the past are almost perceptible. There is a sensation of wide open space that can be both unfamiliar and precious on a crowded island.

Getting there

Scotland's Far North Line trundles along the northeastern coast, with trains serving places such as Helmsdale, Forsinard, Wick and Thurso. Just be ready for slow travel: it's at least an 8hr journey from Edinburgh up to the end of the line at Thurso.

When to go

The shoulder seasons of late spring and early autumn are a great time to visit Scotland's far north; in high summer beware of biting midges and heavy traffic on the North Coast 500 route.

Further reading

Alex Roddie's book *The Farthest Shore* recounts a walk along the Cape Wrath Way.

TOP 10 SUSTAINABLE DESTINATIONS

Spain / Patagonia, Argentina & Chile / Greenland / Wales' Trails
The Portuguese Way / Palau / Hokkaidō, Japan / Ecuador
Baltic Trails / Eco Lodges, South Africa

Spain

SPAIN

One of the globe's most popular destinations, sun-washed Spain is leading the green-travel way with its pioneering plans for a more sustainable, circular tourism model.

Left: the Ciudad de las Artes y las Ciencias abuts the Jardín del Turia

first. Elsewhere, creative small-scale hotels, energetic adventure-activity companies, fresh Vías Verdes (old train lines reborn as cycling and hiking paths) and other initiatives are revitalising the country's less-populated rural areas. Then there's a wave of new train routes making flight-free travel a breeze, including in-the-pipeline high-speed AVE lines for Asturias and the País Vasco (Basque Country).

In recent years, Spain has made big strides to expand renewable energy, boost off-season travel, spread visitors across the year and bring tourism to overlooked destinations. The Mediterranean city of Valencia, named European Green Capital for 2024, is working to become carbon-neutral in tourism by 2025; a raft of new cycle paths, green spaces and electric buses are just a taster of its forward-thinking plans. The Balearic Islands, meanwhile, have introduced tourism restrictions and are prioritising positive-impact trips that put local culture, gastronomy and natural spaces

HIGHLIGHTS

→ Jardín del Turia, Valencia's ingenious transformation of the old Turia riverbed into a 9km-long (5.5-mile) road-free park has created one of Spain's best-loved green lungs and also reduced local traffic; hire a bike or join a two-wheel tour.

Patagonia, Argentina & Chile

ARGENTINA & CHILE

New trails, ever-growing parklands and one of the most ambitious rewilding projects in the Americas make Patagonia both wilder and more approachable than ever before.

On the Argentinian side, Parque Nacional Patagonia will unveil a planetarium and interpretation centre in late 2023 that – alongside new trails past ancient rock-art sites in the Cañadón Río Pinturas – could finally give this remote reserve the star power it deserves.

Meanwhile, a park of the same name just across the border in Chile has successfully rewilded pumas, rheas and endangered huemul deer to steppelands damaged by decades of ranching. That park is but one of 17 that make up Chile's 2800km-long (1740-mile)

Left: Parque Nacional Queulat is one of the 17 reserves on Route of the Parks

Route of the Parks, which covers subantarctic rainforests, vast ice fields and one of the most extensive fjord systems on Earth. The initiative is intended to inspire local people and provide incomes. Need another reason to visit in 2024? An annular solar eclipse will black out the skies over both Patagonia National Parks on October 2, creating even more buzz in one of the planet's wildest corners.

HIGHLIGHTS
→ Visit some of the fast-melting glaciers in Argentina's Parque Nacional Los Glaciares.
→ Take the strain off high-profile trek routes and try the five-day Dientes Circuit, the southernmost hike on Earth.

Greenland

GREENLAND

Greenland's ice and tundra have long intrigued explorers. Increasingly, the world's largest island beckons intrepid travellers, too – and getting there will soon become easier.

Left: The northern lights shimmer above Ilulissat in Greenland on dark nights

hydrophones let travellers and scientists eavesdrop on, and study, Arctic sea life.

Next spring marks the tenth anniversary of Arctic Sounds, a charismatic five-day festival in the west-coast town of Sisimiut.

A pristine northern-lights escape, Greenland will enjoy a spike in aurora sightings as the sun, the catalyst for those coloured ribbons, reaches peak activity in the next few years.

In 2024, Greenland plans to unveil two new international airports: one in the colourful capital Nuuk, the other in Ilulissat. These hubs could foster a long-awaited link between Greenland and North America, and are part of Greenland's plan to create a sustainable economy – one that relies on tourism and fishing, not oil or mining. Nearly 90% of Greenland's population is Inuit; for them, environmental and cultural preservation takes priority. Local travel experiences follow suit. Take Disko LIVE!, the Arctic's first permanent listening station, opening in 2023. Here,

HIGHLIGHTS

→ Scout for the aurora and admire the icescape on a low-impact adventure: Camp Ice Cap, a two-day camping trip on the world's second-largest ice sheet. The trip commences in Kangerlussuaq, just a short drive from the sea of ice.

Wales' Trails

WALES

A rail revamp in Wales – one of the world's first countries to legislate for sustainability – will expand the planet-friendly possibilities of exploring the nation's wild, wonderful west.

Gnarly headlands, boof-ing waves, bird-screeched cliffs, smugglers' coves, spectacular walking trails... Wales' southwest is far less crowded with tourists than the north and has an air of the untouched and untamed. You might assume it's awkward to explore without a car. Not

so. In a country that's serious about sustainability, out-of-the-way Pembrokeshire Coast National Park is quite accessible – and set to get more so. New train stations and increased services are being planned for South Wales' main rail line in early 2025, which could reduce

Left: Hike from bay to bay along the Pembrokeshire Coast Path near St Davids

journey times between London and Carmarthen – gateway to the west – by 20 minutes.

You can visit car-free before then, though. Trains run to hotspots such as Tenby and Fishguard while buses with delightful names – the Puffin Shuttle, the Poppit Rocket – hop along the coast. Use these to plan walks along the Wales Coast Path, the best way to explore this protected shore.

nevereverno/Getty Images/iStockphoto © ↑Michael Roberts/Getty Images ©

HIGHLIGHTS

→ Near St Davids, an ancient farm is now home to Dr Beynon's Bug Farm, a research centre, nature reserve and Grub Kitchen, the UK's first edible-insect cafe. Learn about sustainable food, then tuck into cricket cookies.

The Portuguese Way, Portugal & Spain

More than a pilgrimage route, the Portuguese Way is a scenic journey across Portugal and Spain inviting its visitors to slow down and soak up towns lost to time.

PORTUGAL & SPAIN

Left: The spectacular hilltop basilica of Viana do Castelo dates from 1898

Can't afford a month on the road? The Coastal Way from Porto is a shorter (and flatter) alternative, taking you through wild beaches and historical sites like Viana do Castelo and Valença. Introduced in 2023, the project Caminho da Arte is bringing contemporary artworks to this stretch, with award-winning Portuguese architect Álvaro Siza rolling out the first piece.

Romanesque churches, rivers and ancient villages greet you along the Portuguese Way (Caminho Português de Santiago), a 620km (385-mile) trail linking Lisbon to the pilgrimage site of Santiago de Compostela. You'll spend the night at locally-owned *albergues*, dine in traditional restaurants, and tour small towns that have struggled as their residents flocked to the big cities. Travelling on foot, by bike or train saves on emissions but also allows time to take in the changing scenery and befriend fellow travellers en route.

HIGHLIGHTS

→ Vineyards, medieval towns and upland rivers accompany the Caminho de Torres, an alternative route connecting Salamanca in Spain to northern Portugal.

Palau

PALAU

Combining digital technology and local traditions, a small Pacific nation is leading the way in demonstrating how sustainable travel can alleviate the impact of climate change.

Before Covid-19, tiny Palau – population 18,000 – attracted 90,000 visitors annually, and as the nation rebuilds its tourism industry, a new app will ensure visitors contribute to an ongoing focus on sustainability. Based on how respectfully visitors treat the country's environment, users of Ol'au Palau (olaupalau.com) are rewarded with exclusive experiences. By making choices like using reef-safe sunscreen or eating at local restaurants serving sustainably sourced ingredients, visitors can redeem their points to access cultural and natural experiences usually

Left: The archipelago of Palau is particularly vulnerable to rising sea levels

only available to Palauan families and their friends.

Ol'au Palau is the latest innovation from this global leader in nurturing sustainable tourism. In 2017, the Palau Pledge was launched, linking responsible travel to immigration policy, and requiring visitors to uphold a pledge – stamped into passports on arrival – to protect Palau's culture and natural environment for future generations.

HIGHLIGHTS

→ Experiences with Sam's Tours (samstours.com) are focused on sustainable practices. Offering diving, kayaking, island hikes and sightseeing tours, Sam's has a strict commitment to being a zero-trace tour operator.

Hokkaidō, Japan

Long on the radar of winter sport enthusiasts, Hokkaidō is supporting eco-friendly activities and accommodation, plus a cultural renaissance for the Indigenous Ainu people.

JAPAN

Left: Jōzankei Onsen in Shikotsu-Toya National Park is just an hour from Sapporo

than just increasing numbers of visitors, to the benefit of the whole community. That includes revitalising Ainu language and culture, including music, dance, handicrafts and cuisine.

Six national parks harbour abundant wildlife, excellent hiking trails, steaming hot springs and well-equipped campgrounds. Biking opportunities abound, all over the island. Best of all, there's a real sense of adventure.

With 20% of Japan's land area, but only 5% of its population, Hokkaidō boasts swathes of mountains and wilderness, and once away from the winter resorts, such as Niseko, it's still relatively undiscovered. This is a different side of Japan to that on offer in familiar destinations such as Tokyo, Kyoto and Hiroshima.

Many Japanese dream of exploring Hokkaidō's wide expanses, and the government is hoping to entice more international visitors north, too. The focus is on providing a quality experience, rather

HIGHLIGHTS

→ See traditional Ainu dance and puppet shows at Ikor Theatre in the Ainu *kotan* (village) in Akanko Onsen.

→ Spot a red-crowned crane, a symbol of Japan, in Kushiro-shitsugen National Park.

Ecuador

Home to sprawling rainforests, wild rivers, 20 active volcanoes and an estimated 6% of all species on Earth, megadiverse Ecuador has a lot to protect.

With Ecuador's recent digital nomad visa, visitors can extend a stay in favour of multiple visits. Tourist numbers to the Galápagos are limited to protect the ecosystem, but those who plan ahead will find green operations everywhere, including the world's first renewably powered airport.

The archipelago gets all the attention, but an effort is being made to attract tourism to other areas. The mainland has a further 10 national parks, and part of the mighty Amazon, which is teeming with life and eco-projects deep in the jungle. Meanwhile, many cloud forest accommodations and tropical beach eco-lodges come with their own hydro-schemes and sustainable credentials.

A new marine reserve, Hermandad, will sit north of the Galápagos Islands, and add 52,000 sq km (20,077 sq miles) to the already existing 130,000 sq km (50,193 sq miles) created to protect sea turtles, sharks and other migratory species, forming a Pacific corridor to Costa Rica.

Left: Take a canoe trip to an Indigenous village in Yasuní National Park

HIGHLIGHTS
→ The Napo Wildlife Centre, owned and run by the Añangu Kichwa community, is a stylish Amazonian lodge with compost toilets and solar panels, sitting deep in the jungle of Yasuní National Park.

Baltic Trails

ESTONIA, LATVIA AND LITHUANIA

Treat these paths as Europe's longest meditation practice. Meandering past sand dunes, forests, rivers and lakes is a route towards rediscovering your inner self.

Left: Take a break and breathe deeply on Lithuania's Curonian Spit

of national parks, including the valley of the Gauja River in Latvia, famous for its blazing autumn foliage displays.

For much of the way, you'll feel like you have the entire world to yourself. But on this journey, fuelled by no energy except your own, you also get to see charming log-house villages, quaint historical towns and vibrant metropolitan centres.

The two trails linking the three Baltic states quietly came into being in recent years.

The Baltic Coastal Hiking Route skirts the shores of Estonia, Latvia and Lithuania. It's a virtually uninterrupted display of natural beauty – from the austere Nordic landscapes of Estonia, with giant boulders and waterfalls, to the fine sands of the Curonian Spit in Lithuania, perhaps with some amber hidden within.

The longer Forest Trail cuts through the wooded hinterland. It takes in the placid Lake Peipsi in eastern Estonia and a chain

HIGHLIGHTS

→ Steam off your fatigue in a sauna at the tiny resort of Ziedlejas in the Gauja Valley.

→ Savour herbal tea and onion cakes at Samovar House in a Russian Old Believers' village on Lake Peipsi.

Eco Lodges, South Africa

SOUTH AFRICA

South Africa is an ode to natural grandeur – penguins inhabit the coastline, lions and black rhinos prowl the bush, and the fynbos shrub breathes life into the hills of the Western Cape.

With Earth's biodiversity at a precarious juncture, there's no better time to partake in South Africa's wild beauty, especially with an impressive crop of eco lodges committed to its protection. At the country's southern tip, stay at the awe-inspiring Grootbos Private Nature Reserve, built to blend into the splendid bush landscape. Dine under some of the country's most magnificent (and endangered) milkwood forests, dating back at least 1000 years, and learn about the fascinating world of the endemic fynbos vegetation. Further east, at the

Left: Elephants enjoy the facilities at the Gondwana Game Reserve

conservation-oriented Gondwana Game Reserve, get intimate with the African bush on a three-day walking safari. Take a digital detox as you track the Big Five on foot, accompanied by park rangers who double as master storytellers. Spend star-studded nights with leave-no-trace glamping, and if you're lucky, walk among giraffes and zebras like the humans of yore once did.

Pavel Kuzmichev/Shutterstock © †Raquel De Castro Maia/Courtesy of Gondwana Game Reserve ©

HIGHLIGHTS

→ Book responsible experiences like Lebombo Lodge in Kruger National Park. Avoid places where wild animals are held captive or made to alter their natural behaviour.

TOP 10 BEST VALUE DESTINATIONS

The Midwest, USA / Poland / Nicaragua / Danube Limes, Bulgaria
Normandy, France / Egypt / Ikaria, Greece / Algeria
Southern Lakes & Central Otago, New Zealand / Night Trains, Europe

The Midwest, USA

The American Midwest is unfairly known as that cornfield many people fly over between coasts – but it also holds cities full of creativity, diversity and forking good food.

UNITED STATES

Left: The Mississippi River once powered the flour mills of Minneapolis

enclaves ranging from Somali food in Columbus to Hmong markets in Minneapolis, and you've got reasons enough to visit. But 2024 ups the ante. Cleveland and Indianapolis are prime places to watch the solar eclipse in April, Cuyahoga Valley National Park marks the 50th anniversary of its misty-forest creation, and foodie haven Ann Arbor parties for its 200th birthday all year long.

During the last decade, chefs, artists and designers zipped to cities like Chicago, Milwaukee and Detroit, lured by places that offered plenty of space and let them ply their trade at friendlier costs than on the coasts. Soon, old warehouses transformed into art studios, vacant factories became eco design hotels, and abandoned buildings morphed into Michelin-starred restaurants. Add in the Midwest's world-class museums (including the Art Institute of Chicago and Cleveland's Rock & Roll Hall of Fame), its beer-making legacy, and its cultural

HIGHLIGHTS
→ In Minneapolis, Indigenous-owned Owamni by The Sioux Chef (owamni.com) serves locally sourced, modern Native American fare, with dishes like lake trout, bison stew, wild-rice dumplings and blue corn bread.

Poland

POLAND

From its dynamic and historic cities, stacked with delicious dining options, to its 17 Unesco World Heritage sites and 23 national parks, Poland helps your travel buck go further.

Poland shines as one of Europe's most affordable destinations, offering a superb range of great-value and quality travel experiences. Many visitors gravitate to its thriving cities, like Warsaw, which in 2024 will see the opening of a new complex housing both the Museum of Modern Art and the TR Warszawa Theatre. The capital's culinary scene is also booming, with sophisticated, contemporary dishes using traditional Polish ingredients on the menu at restaurants such as Bez Gwiazdek, Dyletanci and Opasły Tom.

Left: European bison survive in some of Poland's wild forests

Lovers of the outdoors will be thrilled by Polish countryside. In the Carpathian Mountains, hike the Icon Trail, passing through villages graced with old wooden churches. Paddle a kayak across and around the Great Masurian Lakes, or cycle through the World-Heritage-listed Białowieża National Park, a primeval forest that's home to the continent's largest land mammal, the European bison.

↑ CK Foto/Shutterstock © ↑ Mark Read/Lonely Planet ©

HIGHLIGHTS

→ Warsaw's once-abandoned 19th-century Haberbusch & Schiele Brewery has been revived as the social hot spot Browary Warszawskie. Hit up this award-winning complex to enjoy craft beers, culinary treats and cultural events.

Nicaragua

Nicaragua is a beautiful country that can at times be gritty. But it is Central America's top budget destination with surf, sun, colonial villages, tropical forests, lost islands and more.

Left: Relax in the natural splendour of Little Corn Island

reserves. The country continues to recover from a particularly heated bout of civil unrest, natural disasters and other disruptive forces that triggered a significant drop in visitation. With their open hearts and welcoming nature, the warm-spirited people of Nicaragua will be the driving force as the country seeks to reinvent itself in 2024 and welcome visitors back with a warm embrace.

On April 8, 2024, a total solar eclipse will take place across much of North and Central America. Viewing this once-in-a-lifetime spectacle from atop one of Nicaragua's volcanoes might just be the best thing 2024 has to offer. If solar eclipses aren't your thing, there is still plenty to experience cruising the cobblestone streets of Granada, scrambling to the top of the twin volcanoes of Isla de Ometepe, lazing your days away in the surfer villages that dot the Pacific coast, and connecting with the wilds in one of the country's 78 nature

HIGHLIGHTS

→ Off Nicaragua's Caribbean Coast, the Corn Islands move more slowly than the mainland – and that's the way the locals like it. There's no place better to experience this forgotten paradise than the Little Corn Beach and Bungalow.

Danube Limes, Bulgaria

BULGARIA

A string of settlements on the ancient limits of the Roman Empire – known as the Danube Limes – has been nominated for inclusion on the Unesco World Heritage list in 2024.

The structures date from the early centuries of the first millennium CE, as the Roman Empire expanded rapidly along the Danube through parts of modern-day Croatia, Serbia, Romania and Bulgaria. While Unesco protection would extend to settlements in all four countries (joining parts of the Roman limes in Germany, Austria and Slovakia already recognised in 2021), the Bulgarian stretch may be the most impressive. Beginning around the ancient Roman city of Ratiaria, near modern Vidin, and running eastward to the once-mighty fortress at Durostorum (today Silistra) and beyond, the riverbank here is studded with ruins. Some have lain undisturbed since antiquity; others were refurbished and used by conquering Byzantine and Ottoman armies. Many sites can be explored by bike along stages of the Dunav Ultra, a 740km (460-mile) cycling path that follows the Danube to the Black Sea, giving free access for all.

Left: Baba Vida, one of several dramatic fortresses along the Danube River

HIGHLIGHTS

→ Baba Vida is a marvellously preserved medieval castle, built atop the Roman fortress of Bononia, near Vidin. Further east, at Ruse, archeological work is ongoing at the Roman naval base of Sexaginta Prista (Port of 60 Ships).

Normandy, France

In 1872 Monet painted *Sunrise* in the Norman port of Le Havre and two years later Impressionism was born. Now rediscover this venerated region through a new eco-lens.

Left: Claude Monet's house and garden in Giverny is as inspiring as ever

into the heart of a 19th-century movement that turned art on its head with its radical, soulful focus on immortalising outdoor scenes on canvas in a natural, chameleon light. The programme includes open-air theatre performances and dance cafes, art exhibitions and workshops, forest walks, stargazing, sound-and-light shows and romantic picnics à la Renoir. Scores of events are completely free.

Given its proximity to Paris – just over an hour by train from Gare St-Lazare – the meadows, farmsteads and apple orchards of rural Normandy promise an affordable antidote to 2024's Olympic pandemonium in the French capital. But it's not just about slowing down along scenic cycling paths or taking time to learn how third-generation farmers craft camembert and cider. To celebrate 150 years of Impressionism, the region is hosting the Normandy Impressionist Festival (Mar–Sep). This top-billing, multidisciplinary arts festival plunges visitors

HIGHLIGHTS

→ Anne-Christelle and Bertrand ditched the Parisian high life for eco-cabins and a wood-fired Nordic hot tub by a lake and forest at Casa Rosalie (instagram.com/casa_rosalie) in Tourouvre-au-Perche. Expect tranquillity.

Egypt

EGYPT

With Luxor's enigmatic tombs, the timeless essence of the Nile and the mighty Pyramids of Giza, Egypt has a bounty of historical riches that don't cost a fortune to visit.

History is never in the past in Egypt, and new discoveries of gold-laden mummies and forgotten cities continue to make headlines. Ready to show off the country's treasures, the long-anticipated Grand Egyptian Museum is expected to have its doors open by 2024.

While flights to the Egyptian capital tend to be expensive, budget airlines have flown for years to resort towns on the Red Sea coast, sun-and-sand staples for Europeans. Ryanair, Europe's largest budget airline, is rumoured to be starting service to Egypt for the first time, and

Left: Admire the ruins and statues of the Temple of Karnak in Luxor

Air Sphinx, a new low-cost arm of the country's flagship carrier, is also expected to take flight soon.

Economic woes continue to devalue the country's currency, resulting in more savings for foreign travellers, but bringing dire consequences for Egyptians, one-third of whom live in poverty. Keep your spending in the country by arranging tours with local guides and staying in smaller guesthouses and hotels.

↑ Andre Quinou/Shutterstock © ↑ Peter Seaward/Shutterstock ©

HIGHLIGHTS
→ Experience a priceless connection with another side of Egypt's heritage on the Sinai Trail and Red Sea Mountain Trail, two long-distance hiking routes founded by a collective of Bedouin tribes.

Ikaria, Greece

GREECE

The Greek island of Ikaria seduces with aquamarine waters and wild terrain, plus an independent spirit and a culture that includes rock dwellings and rave-like *panigyria* festivals.

Left: Slow down and watch the fishing boats come and go in Evdilos port

than now to enjoy the island's serenity and attitude to life, which results in extraordinary longevity – islanders have one of the highest life expectancy rates in Europe (one in three live into their 90s). Get a taste of their magic recipe, and it's super-affordable, too: long afternoon naps, lots of mountain tea and beans, little coffee and meat, and healthy sex lives into their 80s.

Named after Icarus, who is said to have crashed here after flying too close to the sun with his wax wings, Ikaria is also honoured as the birthplace of Dionysos, god of wine. You can now drive on a paved coastal road all around the island, where Ikarian villages famously throw wild rumpuses brimming with food, wine and traditional dance. Join the party in 2024 at the height of summer's *panigyria*, all-night festival celebrations held on saints' days, and bask in the return to streets packed with visitors and locals alike. There's also no better time

HIGHLIGHTS

→ Seychelles Beach has marble pebbles, emerald water and giant rocks polished by the waves.

→ Spilaio Hot Springs is one of the Aegean's best: radon-rich waters lead to a cave.

Algeria

ALGERIA

A three-hour flight or less from much of Europe, Algeria is one of the most exciting short-haul destinations for adventurous travellers.

You'll find untouristed train journeys, well-preserved Roman sites and fine historic cities, of which the most extraordinary are the pastel-coloured hilltop citadels of the M'Zab Valley, which have banned the selfie in order to avoid becoming yet another 'most-Instagrammable'

destination. But Algeria's undoubted scene-stealer is the Sahara Desert. This mind-bending panorama of rock cathedrals, sand seas and weathered canyonlands stretches for some 1610km (1000 miles), reaching its crescendo in Tassili N'Ajjer, home to Tuareg nomadic

Left: Hike among the rock formations of Tassili N'Ajjer with a Tuareg guide

culture and one of the world's greatest collections of rock art. At times, the bureaucratic hurdles to enter Algeria might seem equally prehistoric, but it's largely back on the safe-to-visit list, and for those willing to persevere, the reward is immense: an affordable, crowd-free experience and some of the most spectacular sights anywhere on the African continent.

† Lemonakis Antonis/Shutterstock © † Hamdi Oussama/Shutterstock ©

HIGHLIGHTS

→ To witness the Algerian Sahara's most beautiful sand dunes, head to the blood-red oasis city of Timimoun and its nearby Grand Erg Occidental, a dune sea twice the size of Belgium.

Southern Lakes & Central Otago

Kiwis have gone biking mad. Restricted to exploring their own backyard during the pandemic, they're pedalling all over their Pacific paradise on a growing number of cycling trails.

NEW ZEALAND

Left: Riding the 15km (nine-mile) Glendhu Bay track beside Lake Wānaka

Wānaka has wonderful lakeside rides; and Central Otago is seeing formerly sleepy towns revitalised, such as Clyde, at the end of the recently opened 55km (34-mile) Lake Dunstan Trail. In a few years, bikers will be able to ride from Queenstown and Wānaka all the way through Central Otago to Dunedin on the east coast.

In an area best-known for its golf courses, winter sports and wineries, activities such as biking, hiking and exploring the outdoors are free and accessible to all around New Zealand's popular Southern Lakes resorts of Queenstown and Wānaka, as well as in Central Otago.

When it comes to biking, new trails are being opened, more being constructed and bigger plans are afoot. While locals are in the know, international visitors have barely cottoned on.

The Queenstown Trails Network comprises over 130km (80 miles) of bike trails;

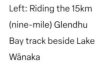

HIGHLIGHTS

→ Park your bike in the rack and savour a craft beer from Altitude Brewery, along with cheap eats, at Atlas Beer Cafe in Queenstown, an affordable hotspot that's popular with with local bikers.

Night Trains, Europe

EUROPE

After decades of decline, Europe's sleeper trains are undergoing a renaissance – thanks to travellers who want to keep CO2 emissions down and watch the world speed by.

Not long ago, it seemed like the end of the line for Europe's night trains – budget airlines and newer, faster high-speed rail services had done much to diminish the appeal of bedding down in a compartment, and snoozing to the slow lullaby of clanking rails. Now – in the age of carbon-conscious travel – that's changing. Austrian Federal Railways' (ÖBB) Nightjet brand has been leading the charge, establishing a number of new routes across Central Europe. There's evidence, too, of private companies taking the initiative: European Sleeper intends to connect Amsterdam with Barcelona in the near future, while French outfit Midnight Trains is planning to wholly reinvent the sleeper train experience, creating carriages designed like luxury hotels. It seems Europe is waking up to the potential of sleeper trains, and the small wonder of dozing off and coming around to a new destination the next morning.

Left: Nightjet's sleeper services cover Germany, Italy and beyond

↑Janice Chen/Shutterstock © ↑Harald Eisenberger/Courtesy of Nightjet ©

HIGHLIGHTS

→ Of all the new sleeper routes, arguably the most exciting is the Brussels–Prague service, slowly being rolled out by Dutch-Belgian company European Sleeper, with stops in Amsterdam, Berlin and Dresden along the way.

INDEX

MAKING BEST IN TRAVEL

Of all the amazing places and travel experiences on the planet, how do we choose the most exciting for the year ahead? It's a decision we do not take lightly. Read on for an overview of how the magic happens.

① THE SURVEY

The annual *Best in Travel* survey is sent to the whole Lonely Planet family – every staff member, over 200 travel writers, bloggers, our publishing partners and more. In it we ask them to share their expertise on places and travel experiences that they predict will be buzzing in the year ahead.

② THE TRAVEL HACK

In a typical year, we organise brainstorming events in Lonely Planet offices the world over, from Beijīng to Buenos Aires. This is when we come together to discuss the subject that inspires us the most: travel. Zoom calls were the substitute this year but the questions were the same. What are we excited about? Which destinations are doing something special? And where do we want to visit next?

③ SHORTLISTING

The results of the survey and Travel Hacks produce a longlist of more than a thousand ideas. This is then reviewed by Lonely Planet's *Best in Travel* team – an opinionated bunch of travel geeks with hundreds of thousands of travel miles between them. The team read every pitch and help whittle down the list to a shortlist of the very best places.

④ THE PANEL

The shortlist is then sent to a panel of travel experts: seven people who live and breathe travel with a wide range of specialist knowledge. They scrutinise each idea and score them out of 10 for topicality, uniqueness and, this year, whether they warranted a place in our 50th anniversary edition of Best in Travel. This year our panel included travel writers Kelsy Chauvin, Tharik Hussain, Cory Lee, Shivya Nath and Monisha Rajesh; Melanie Lieberman, a Senior Editor at Thepointsguy. com and Nitya Chambers, Senior Vice President of Content and Executive Editor at Lonely Planet.

⑤ THE FINAL LIST

When the panel results are in, the list is finalised and shared with a trusted handful of people at Lonely Planet until October when, finally, the selection of the best places and travel experiences for the year ahead is shared with the world.

Best in Travel 2024
October 2023
Published by Lonely Planet Global Limited
CRN 554153
www.lonelyplanet.com
1 2 3 4 5 6 7 8 9 10

Publishing Director Piers Pickard
Publisher Becca Hunt
Senior Editor Robin Barton
Editors Rory Goulding, Polly Thomas
Layout Designers Daniel Di Paolo, Lauren Egan, Emily Dubin
Print Production Nigel Longuet

Brett Atkinson (Palau), Alexis Averbuck (Ikaria), Mark Baker (Prague; Danube Limes), Joel Balsam (Morocco), Sarah Baxter (Wales' Trails), Greg Benchwick (Nicaragua), Joe Bindloss (India; Pakistan), Jade Bremner (Ecuador; Jakarta), Alex Crevar (Trans Dinarica Cycling Route), Kathy Donaghy (Donegal), Peter Dragicevich (Croatia), Mary Fitzpatrick (Swahili Coast), Lucie Grace (Mostar), Jen Hattam (İzmir), John Hecht (Mexico), Carolyn Heller (Montréal), Tharik Hussain (Southern Thailand), Mark Johanson (Chile; Patagonia), Lauren Keith (Egypt; Kansas City), Michael Kohn (Mongolia), Abbie Kozolchyk (Philadelphia), Stephen Lioy (Uzbekistan), Craig McLachlan (Hokkaidō; Southern Lakes & Central Otago), Shivya Nath (South Africa), Isabella Noble (País Vasco; Spain), Nanjala Nyabola (Nairobi), Leonid Ragozin (Baltic Trails), Kevin Raub (Manaus), Simon Richmond (Poland), Noo Saro-Wiwa (Benin), Maggie Slepian (Montana), Oliver Smith (Far North Scotland; Night Trains, Europe), Nasha Smith (St Lucia), Joana Taborda (The Portuguese Way), Simon Urwin (Algeria), Stephanie Vermillion (Greenland), Kerry Walker (Saalfelden Leogang), Nicola Williams (Paris; Tuscany; Normandy), Chris Zeiher (Kangaroo Island), Karla Zimmerman (The Midwest), Tom Hall (Introduction)

Printed in Malaysia
ISBN 9781837581061
© Lonely Planet 2023
© photographers as indicated 2023
Front cover photos by Carolinie Cavalli, Meiying Ng, Simon Berger, Yuriy Kovalev on Unsplash.
Back cover photos: Kerala, India © rchphoto / Getty Images; Arc de Triumph, Paris © iDrone Aerials / Shutterstock; Leongang, Austria © Eder / Shutterstock.

Lonely Planet Global Limited

Digital Depot, Roe Lane (off Thomas St), Digital Hub, Dublin 8, D08 TCV4 Ireland

STAY IN TOUCH
lonelyplanet.com/contact